KT-227-852

Essential
Mallorca

by Tony Kelly

Tony Kelly took up travel writing after
teaching English in Sudan and China.
He writes regularly for newspapers
and magazines, specialising in walking and
the outdoors. When not travelling he
lives on a farm in eastern England with
his wife and young son.
This is his first guidebook.

AA Publishing

SANTA CATALINA THOMAS PREGAU PER NOSALTRES

Page 1: *Cala Sant Vicenç*

Page 5a: *Green shutters, Cala Santanyí;*
5b: *Old timer in local café in Muro*

Page15a: *Narrow streets of Valldemossa;*
15b: *Detail on Portal del Mirador, La Seu*

Page 27a: *Hairpin bends on the way down to Sa Calobra;*
27b: *Monument, Santa Ponça*

Page 91a: *Floorshow at Casino Mallorca;*
91b: *Wall plaque in Palma*

Page 117a: *Windmill at Algaida;*
117b: *Sóller oranges*

Find out more about AA Publishing and the wide range of services the AA provides by visiting our Web site at www.theaa.co.uk.

Written by Tony Kelly

Edited, designed and produced by AA Publishing.
© The Automobile Association 1998
Maps © The Automobile Association 1998

Distributed in the United Kingdom by AA Publishing, Norfolk House, Priestley Road, Basingstoke, Hampshire, RG24 9NY.

A CIP catalogue record for this book is available from the British Library.

ISBN 0 7495 1223 7

Published by AA Publishing, a trading name of Automobile Association Developments Limited, whose registered office is Norfolk House, Priestley Road, Basingstoke, Hampshire, RG24 9NY.
Registered number 1878835.

Colour separation: BTB Digital Imaging, Whitchurch, Hampshire

Printed and bound in Italy by Printer Trento srl

Contents

About this Book

KEY TO SYMBOLS

✠ map reference to the maps found in the What to See section (see below)

✉ address or location

☎ telephone number

🕓 opening times

🍴 restaurant or café on premises or near by

Ⓜ nearest underground train station

🚍 nearest bus/tram route

🚆 nearest overground train station

⛴ ferry crossings and excursions by boat

✈ travel by air

ℹ tourist information

♿ facilities for visitors with disabilities

✋ admission charge

↔ other places of interest near by

❓ other practical information

▶ indicates the page where you will find a fuller description

---

Essential *Mallorca* is divided into five sections to cover the most important aspects of your visit to Mallorca.

Viewing Mallorca pages 5–14
An introduction to Mallorca by the author.
Mallorca's Features
Essence of Mallorca
The Shaping of Mallorca
Peace and Quiet
Mallorca's Famous

Top Ten pages 15–26
The author's choice of the Top Ten places to visit in Mallorca, with practical information.

What to See pages 27–90
Alphabetical listings of the main attractions in Palma and around the island.
Practical information
Snippets of 'Did You Know…' information
4 suggested walks
4 suggested tours
2 features

Where To… pages 91–116
Detailed listings of the best places to eat, stay, shop, take the children and be entertained.

Practical Matters pages 117–24
A highly visual section containing essential travel information.

Maps
All map references are to the individual maps in the What to See section of this guide. For example, La Seu in Palma has the reference ✠ 35B2 – indicating the page on which the map is located and the grid square in which the cathedral is to be found. A list of the maps that have been used in this travel guide can be found in the index. As with the maps, place-names in the text are given in Catalan; where a Spanish word or phrase is more widely used, that is given instead.

Prices
Where appropriate, an indication of the cost of an establishment is given by £ signs: £££ denotes higher prices, ££ denotes average prices, while £ denotes lower charges.

Star Ratings
Most of the places described in this book have been given a separate rating:
✪✪✪   Do not miss
✪✪   Highly recommended
✪   Worth seeing

Viewing
Mallorca

Tony Kelly's Mallorca

Mallorca or Majorca?
Are they the same place or
not? Yes and no. Majorca,
with a hard 'j', is a place
invented by foreigners, where
the sun always shines, the
beer flows and the nearest
you get to local culture is an
argument with a taxi-driver.
Mallorca, the local name for
the island, is somewhere
quite different and far more
complex. This book is about
Mallorca.

Sheep with bells around their necks grazing beneath olive trees; hilltop sanctuaries where you spend the night in what was once a monk's cell. These are probably not your typical images of Mallorca.

If you thought Mallorca was all sweaty bodies, in the disco and on the beach, think again. It is that, of course - that's the main reason why 6 million tourists visit the island every year. But there is an awful lot more to Mallorca than sun, sea and sand.

Whisper it gently, but Mallorca is changing its image. Fed up with being labelled cheap and cheerful, it has gone for a new approach. High-rise apartment blocks are being torn down, to be replaced by tree-lined promenades. Manor houses and country estates are being converted into stylish hotels. Tourists are encouraged to come in winter, to walk, cycle and play golf. The island that led the way into mass tourism is now leading the way out.

Not just land and sea – Mallorca is starting to attract walkers and cyclists

For such a small island, the variations are extraordinary. You can spend one day lying on the beach, the next walking in the mountains. Castles, caves, countryside, hidden coves... whatever you want from a holiday, it is probably there. Except, perhaps, snow.

Of course there is nowhere in Mallorca still waiting to be 'discovered' – even the tiniest villages are heavily dependent on tourism. But strike off the main roads and into the small towns on the plain, simply go wherever you see a cluster of brown houses on a hill, and you will find a Mallorca utterly at odds with the familiar image.

Mallorca's Features

Geography

• Mallorca is the largest of the Balearic islands, a group that includes Menorca, Ibiza and Formentera.

• Mallorca measures 100km from east to west and 75km from north to south.

• Mallorca lies 200km south of Barcelona off the east coast of Spain.

• Mallorca has 555km of coastline and 75 beaches.

• The rocky islands Cabrera and Sa Dragonera provide havens for nesting seabirds.

• The Serra de Tramuntana and Serra de Llevant are two mountain ranges divided by a fertile central plain.

• Palma has an average daily maximum temperature of 21.4°C and an average of seven hours of sunshine per day throughout the year.

Pine-clad cliffs lean into the sea along the spectacular north coast

Tourism

• Mallorca received 1 million tourists in 1966, 3 million in 1978 and 6 million in 1995. In 1995, 40% of visitors were German, 27% were British and 10% were from mainland Spain.

• On busy days in summer up to 700 flights land at Palma airport, carrying up to 100,000 passengers.

• Mallorca has 200,000 hotel beds and 60,000 in tourist apartments.

• Mallorca has enough restaurant tables for a quarter of the population to eat out every night.

• Mallorca's GDP (Gross Domestic Product) per capita is more than 50% above the Spanish average. Two-thirds of the population work in tourism, which represents about 60% of GDP.

Language

• The official languages are Catalan and Castilian Spanish, though Catalan has enjoyed a strong revival in recent years and is now the preferred language in education and local government.

• Most people speak Mallorquín, a dialect of Catalan.

People

Of 630,000 people in Mallorca, half live in the capital Palma. The next biggest towns are Manacor (30,000) and Inca (22,000). The population has doubled since 1950 and includes a large number of expatriates – around 30,000 Germans and almost as many British.

7

Essence of Mallorca

Mallorca's character is shaped, above all, by its climate. The people of the Mediterranean know how to take life slowly – they still have time to sit in the shade and chat, to take a siesta rather than rushing back to work, to enjoy the outdoors whether it is the mountains or the sea.

The warm climate has long attracted outsiders, whose influence can still be felt; Romans, Arabs and Europeans have all left their mark on Mallorca's landscape and culture. But what have not changed are the enduring values of an island people, courteous, proud and self-sufficient.

Aquarium at Porto Cristo (above); fisherman at Port de Sóller (below); the dubious attractions of Platja de Palma (right)

THE **10** ESSENTIALS

If you only have a short time to visit Mallorca, or would like to get a really complete picture of the country, here are the essentials:

• **Spend a day in Palma** exploring the old city, then join the evening *passeig* along the waterfront for a drink in one of the island's trendiest bars (➤ 30–40).

• **Take the joyride to Sóller** on a vintage electric train through the mountains (➤ 71).
• **Enjoy a boat trip** around the coast, passing hidden coves which you cannot reach in a car.
• **Walk in the Serra de Tramuntana** (➤ 83–4), breathing in the heady mix of fresh air, sea breeze and scented wild herbs.
• **Sit at a quayside restaurant** eating fresh fish – choose from any one of the island's ports (➤ 92–9).

Take the tram to Port de Sóller and the boat to Sa Calobra – or spend the day working on your tan

• **Visit the monastery at Valldemossa** where Chopin and George Sand spent the winter of 1838–9 (➤ 26).
• **Drive (or walk) to a hilltop sanctuary** to experience 'the other Mallorca' – if you really want to get away from it all, spend the night.
• **Visit the traditional market at Sineu** (➤ 86) to haggle over everything from sausages to sheep.
• **Get a tan on a crowded beach** – you haven't 'done' Mallorca until you have.
• **Find out where there is a local festival going on** (➤ 116) – and drop everything to get there.

The Shaping of Mallorca

5000 BC
Evidence of human habitation in caves on the north coast.

1300–800 BC
The Talaiotic culture creates settlements like those at Artà and Capocorb Vell.

400 BC
First references to *honderos* (Balearic slingers) fighting in the Punic Wars.

123 BC
The island is conquered by the Romans, who name it Balearis Major, introduce vineyards and olives, and establish their capital at Pollentia, now Alcúdia.

AD 426
Vandal invasion leads to persecution of Christians.

534
Byzantine conquest restores Christianity and brings Mallorca into the province of Sardinia.

902
Arab invasion – Mallorca enters the Caliphate of Córdoba. Oranges and almonds are introduced, along with windmills and irrigation techniques. Palma, known as Medina Mayurqa, is the envy of Europe, with street lights and heated baths.

1229
The origins of modern Mallorca – the conquest by Jaume I of Aragón. Catalan becomes the main language.

1275
Ramón Llull establishes his first hermitage at Puig de Randa.

1276
On Jaume I's death, his kingdom is divided up and his son Jaume II becomes the first King of Mallorca.

1276–1349
The 'Golden Age of Independence' – the building of Castell de Bellver, Palau de l'Almudaina and Alcúdia's city walls.

1349
Jaume III is killed at Llucmajor and Mallorca's independence ends when the island is reincorporated into Aragón.

1492
Modern Spain is created with the union of Aragón, Castile and Granada.

16th–18th Centuries
Repeated pirate attacks lead to the building of watchtowers around the coast.

1715
After victory in the War of the Spanish Succession, Felipe V imposes central rule and the Castilian language on the island of Mallorca.

Statue of Ramón Llull on the waterfront at Palma

10

1836
Opening of a steamer service between Mallorca and Spain.

1879–98
Period of 'gold fever' due to the booming export trade in wine and almonds – until the vines are destroyed by the phylloxera virus, leading to mass emigration.

1902–3
The Gran Hotel opens in Palma. Thomas Cook runs its first tours to Mallorca.

1905
Founding of the Fomento del Turismo de Mallorca (tourist board).

1929
Opening of the Hotel Formentor.

1936–9
The Spanish Civil War, followed by dictatorship under General Franco.

1950
The first charter flight lands in Mallorca.

1960
The opening of Son Sant Joan airport leads to the start of the tourist boom.

1966
Mallorca receives a million tourists.

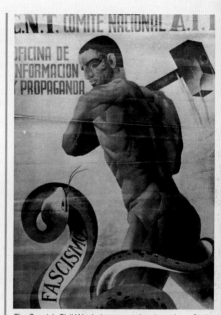

The Spanish Civil War led to repression throughout Spain

1975
Death of Franco and restoration of the monarchy.

1978
A new constitution grants limited autonomy to the Spanish regions.

1983
The Balearic Islands become an autonomous region with their capital at Palma. Catalan becomes the official language.

1984
Opening of La Residencia hotel in Deià.

1986
Spain joins the European Community.

1988
A new coastal law prohibits further development within 100m of the sea.

1995
Mallorca receives 6 million tourists.

1997
The new terminal at Son Sant Joan airport comes into operation, increasing capacity to 27 million passengers a year.

Peace & Quiet

Olive trees near Andratx – it is still surprisingly easy to get away from it all in Mallorca

If you want peace and quiet in Mallorca, go in winter – only 10 per cent of foreign tourists visit between November and March. The island is particularly beautiful in February, when almond blossom carpets the ground like snow. Even in the height of summer, there are plenty of opportunities to escape the crowds. Half of the locals live in Palma, and 90 per cent of the tourists stay on a few small stretches of coast – which leaves large areas of Mallorca just waiting to be explored.

Rights of Way
Walkers have the right of way on all coastal paths, plus routes to miradors, monasteries and mountain peaks (except Puig Major). In recent years, many landowners have attempted to deny access by erecting 'private' signs. If challenged, just state clearly where you are going.

Walking

The obvious areas are the mountains, especially the Serra de Tramuntana (▶ 83–4). At the lower levels, up to around 700m, you walk through *garrigue*, a typical Mediterranean landscape where Aleppo pines mix with wild olives and the stony ground sprouts beautiful wild flowers – orchids and peonies and cistus and asphodel – in spring. (Spring here arrives early, from late February through to May.) Higher up, you reach the *maquis* scrubland, where little grows apart from thorny bushes of heather, bracken, rosemary and broom. Above 1,000m the land is barren – but the views from this height are magnificent and the sense of isolation complete.

Take sensible precautions when walking in the mountains – good boots, extra clothing, food and water, a map, compass and whistle. If you prefer more gentle walks, just strike out along any of the minor roads between the small towns on the plain, or follow a coastal footpath to find your own private bay.

Birds

Mallorca is a paradise for birdwatchers, who come from all over Europe each spring and autumn to see migrating birds on their way to and from wintering in Africa. The best times are April to May and September to October, and the best areas are S'Albufera (▶ 77) and the Salines de Llevant near Ses Salines (▶ 85). The reedbeds of S'Albufera come alive each spring with the song of herons and warblers; other species include egrets, terns, hoopoes, sandpipers and woodcat shrike. Numerous wading birds and wildfowl are attracted to the salt marshes at Ses Salines, including plovers, stilts, water rails and black-tailed godwits. Good spots for watching seabirds include Cap de Ses Salines on the south coast and Cap de Formentor in the northeast (▶ 18), where shags and shearwaters nestle on the cliffs.

Birds of Prey

The mountains of the Serra de Tramuntana are a haven for birds of prey, including ospreys, peregrines, Montagu's harriers and Eleanora's falcons. Rarest of all are the black vultures, of which only a few dozen remain in the area around Lluc monastery. An exhibition at the monastery describes a conservation programme to protect both these and another endangered species, the Mallorcan midwife toad. The best places to see black vultures, and other predatory birds, are at the Cúber and Gorg Blau reservoirs on the road through the mountains from Lluc to Sóller.

The moutain ranges of Mallorca are one of the last remaining European habitats of the black vulture

Mallorca's Famous

Richard Branson (1950–)
The British entrepreneur, owner of Virgin airlines, has long had a reputation for spotting a trend in the market before it happens. So when he opened La Residencia hotel in Deià in 1984, the word was out – Mallorca must be moving up-market. A frequent visitor to Mallorca, he recently acquired a second estate near Banyalbufar. Watch this space...

Ramón Llull

Ramón Llull (1235–1316) was a wealthy courtier in Palma until a disastrous seduction attempt (► 75) led him to retire to Puig de Randa in isolation. Devoting himself to prayer and study, he wrote in Catalan and Latin on everything from algebra to metaphysics; he is widely seen as the father of the Catalan language. Recalled to the court by Jaume II, he established an Oriental language school at Valldemossa and learnt Arabic with the help of a Moorish slave. He was stoned to death attempting to convert Muslims in Tunisia.

Junípero Serra

The Mallorcan missionary, Junípero Serra (1713–84), is honoured in the Capitol in Washington as 'the founder of California'. Of course California was there already; but it was Serra, sent there at the age of 54 after 14 years in Mexico, who established the missions which have grown into some of America's biggest cities, including San Diego and San Francisco. A museum in his home town of Petra (► 64) tells the story. He was beatified in 1988, the first step on the road to sainthood.

Joan Miró

Though not strictly Mallorcan, Joan Miró (1893–1983), the Catalan artist, spent the last 27 years of his life in Mallorca and the islanders have adopted him as their own. His bright, surreal designs adorn everything from tourist posters (the widely used España and Mallorca logos are his) to T-shirts and the mural in the Parc de la Mar in Palma. His house and studio near Palma have been turned into a gallery of his work (► 56).

Statue of Junípero Serra in Palma (above); Joan Miró at work (right)

Top Ten

1
Alcúdia

29D5

Choice of restaurants and bars (£–££)

From Palma/Port d'Alcúdia

Port d'Alcúdia (➤ 67)

Market held Tue & Sun

Museu Monogràfic de Pollentia

Carrer Sant Jaume 30

546413

Apr–Oct, Tue–Sat 10–1:30, 5:30–8, Sun 10–1:30; Nov–Mar, Tue–Sun 10:30–2

Cheap

Roman Remains

Open access

Portal del Moll, once the gateway to Alcúdia from its port, leads directly into the heart of the city

A perfectly restored walled city on the site of a Roman settlement, with remains of Roman houses and an amphitheatre.

This is a gem of a place, a maze of narrow streets enclosed by medieval ramparts, carefully restored as a model of Mallorca's new tourist image. There were Phoenician and Greek settlements here, but the town reached its heyday in the 2nd century BC, when the Roman invaders made it their capital, Pollentia, meaning 'power'. Destroyed by Vandals in the 6th century, the town returned to greatness under the Moors, who built *al-kudia* ('the town on the hill'). The walls you see today were added after the Spanish conquest in the 14th century.

You enter the city through one of the two town gates – the Portal del Moll, with two square towers and two massive palm trees standing guard, is the symbol of Alcúdia. The narrow streets of the old town, especially Carrer d'en Serra, are resonant of Palma's Arab quarter. Look for the Ca'n Torro library, at Carrer d'en Serra 15, opened in 1990 in a former mansion.

A short walk from the parish church of Sant Jaume takes you to three interesting sights, connected by signposted footpaths. Closest to town are the remains of Roman houses at Pollentia; near here are the well-preserved **Teatro Romano** (Roman amphitheatre), and the Oratori de Santa Anna, one of Mallorca's oldest churches. After exploring the Roman remains, interpret them at the **Museu Monogràfic de Pollentia** beside the parish church.

2
Badia de Palma
(Palma Bay)

*The good, the bad and the ugly sides
of Mallorca's tourist development meet along
a 25-km stretch of coast.*

✚ 28B3

🍴 Numerous bars and
restaurants in all the
resorts (£)

🚌 From Palma to all the
resorts

The former villages of S'Arenal and Magaluf sit facing each other across Palma Bay. Once upon a time, a fisherman casting his net into the sea at S'Arenal could have gazed around an empty coastline where the only buildings to stand out would have been Palma's cathedral and castle. Nowadays he would barely be able to distinguish them among a continuous stretch of hotels, a concrete jungle extending all the way to Magaluf. And he wouldn't be there anyway as there are few fish left to catch.

Like it or loathe it, you are bound to spend some time in Palma Bay – even if you are not staying here, you should visit at least once to see some of the best, and the worst, that Mallorca has to offer. Each of the

resorts (described separately in the What To See section) has its own character – young or old, British or German, cheap-and-cheerful or jet-set rich. One moment you can be in Portals Nous, with its chic marina crammed with millionaires' yachts (you have to be seriously rich just to look at the restaurant menus here), the next in seedy Magaluf, all British pubs and wet T-shirt contests.

Occasionally you come across a glimpse of what this coastline must once have been like. Follow the road beyond Magaluf through the pine woods. Suddenly you are among tiny coves where, out of season, you might still find your own private beach. Eventually you reach the headland of Cap de Cala Figuera where you can look back at sweeping views of the entire bay. Cliffs plunge into the clear blue sea, with not a hotel in sight. Come up here at midnight for utter peace and solitude; but listen carefully and you might just be able to hear the disco beat of Magaluf pounding away beneath you.

🚢 Boat tours of Palma Bay
in summer from Palma,
S'Arenal, Palma Nova
and Magaluf

♿ Level beach promenades
at Platja de Palma and
Magaluf

↔ Cala Major (▶ 47),
Magaluf (▶ 59), Palma
Nova (▶ 63), Platja de
Palma (▶ 64), Portals
Nous (▶ 72), Portals
Vells (▶ 72), Ses Illetes
(▶ 85)

*Sun, sea and sand but
little solitude – resorts like
Magaluf epitomise the
growth of Mallorcan
tourism*

17

3
Cap de Formentor

🔲 29E5

🍴 Café with snacks at Cap de Formentor (£); restaurant (£££) in Hotel Formentor

🚌 From Palma and Port de Pollença in summer

⛴ From Port de Pollença to Formentor beach and Cap de Formentor in summer

❓ The best time to see birds and flowers is spring

There are several opportunities to stop and admire the view along the twisting road to Cap de Formentor

This wild peninsula on Mallorca's northeast tip has stunning views, sandy beaches and the island's original luxury hotel.

The 20-km drive from Port de Pollença to Mallorca's most northerly point has scenery as dramatic as anyone could wish for. Cliffs 400m tall jut into the sea, their weird rock formations attracting nesting seabirds, while pine trees seem to grow out of the rocks. The drive is also famously scary – a local legend has it that the parish priest and the local bus driver arrived at the Pearly Gates, and only the driver was admitted to heaven. The reason? He had led far more people to pray.

Six kilometres from Port de Pollença you reach the Mirador des Colomer – scramble up the steps for views over a rocky islet. A path opposite the steps leads to an old watchtower from which you can see the whole of the peninsula as well as the bays of Pollença and Alcúdia. The road continues through pine woods and past more *miradors* (each one helpfully indicated with a picture of an old-fashioned camera) before tunnelling through En Fumat mountain, where you look down over Mallorca's most inaccessible beach. Eventually you reach a lighthouse with the inevitable bar and shop and more stunning views, all the way to Menorca on a good day.

On the way back, stop at Formentor beach and the Hotel Formentor, which opened in 1929 and has been pampering the rich and famous ever since. The fine sandy beach used to be reserved for the hotel's guests, but democracy has opened it to the masses.

4
Castell d'Alaró

*A popular walk to a ruined castle and
hilltop chapel offering spectacular views all
the way to the sea.*

A castle has stood on this site since Moorish times; it was
so impregnable that the Arab commander was able to hold
out for two years after the Christian conquest. Later, in
1285, two heroes of Mallorcan independence, Cabrit and
Brassa, defended the castle against Alfonsó III of Aragón
and were burned alive on a spit when he finally took it by
storm. Their punishment was a consequence of their
impudent defiance of the king. They pretended to confuse
Alfonso's name with that of a local fish – *anfós*, shouting:
'We like our *anfós* grilled.' The present ruins date from the
15th century and seem almost to grow out of the rock,
dominating the landscape for miles around.

The climb up here is one of Mallorca's most popular
walks; do not go on a Sunday
if you want to be alone. From
the town of Alaró it takes
about two hours, following
the signs from the PM210 to
Orient; you can also leave
from Orient (▶ 63), following
a small path opposite
L'Hermitage hotel, again
taking around two hours in
total. The paths converge at
Es Verger restaurant (you
can even bring a car this far
if you don't mind the potholes
and the hairpin bends),
where you can fill up with
roast lamb to fortify you for
the final steep climb.

At last you reach the
castle, 800m above sea
level; look back at the view,
stretching across the entire
plain to Palma and out to
sea. A few minutes further
brings you to the summit,
with a small chapel and
sanctuary, and (bliss!) a
restaurant and bar. If you are
inspired by the views, you
can stay the night here in
one of the simple rooms.

✝ 28C4

☎ Sanctuary: 510480

🕐 Open access

🍴 Es Verger (££) on the
way up; simple
restaurant (££) at the
sanctuary

🚌 From Palma to Alaró

↔ Orient (▶ 63)

*The final steps of the
climb – almost time for a
well-earned drink at the
hilltop bar*

5
Castell de Bellver

✝ 28B3

✉ Parc Bellver

☎ 730657

🕐 Apr–Sep, daily 8–7:30;
Nov–Mar, daily 8–5:30

🚌 3 or 21 to Plaça Gomila

✋ Cheap. Free entrance on
Sun, when museum
closed

❓ Evening concerts in Jul
& Aug

A well-preserved 14th-century royal fortress with fragrant pine woods, an interesting museum and superb views over Palma Bay.

Looking up at this castle, so perfectly maintained, it is hard to believe that it has been standing for almost 700 years. Begun by Jaume II in 1300 and built by Pere Salvà, the architect of the Almudaina Palace, it is unique among Spanish castles in being entirely round. Three large towers surround a central courtyard, connected by an arch to a free-standing keep. The courtyard itself is on two levels, the ground floor with semicircular arches and a flat roof, the upper level with Gothic arches and rib-vaulting. For the full effect, walk around the moat then climb onto the roof and look down into the courtyard to compare the contrasting styles. While you are there, look out over the city and the bay for one of the best views in Palma (Bellver means 'lovely view' in Catalan).

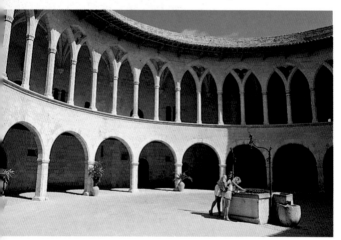

Bellver Castle has been both a royal residence and a military prison, but its main function now is as a historical museum

For many centuries the castle was used as a prison; Jaume III's widow and sons were imprisoned here for most of their lives. These days it contains Palma's museum of municipal history which traces the development of the city through its artefacts, with pottery from Talaiotic, Roman, Arab and Spanish periods.

You can get there by car or taxi, or take a bus to Plaça Gomila and climb up through the pine woods above Carrer de Bellver, passing a chapel on the way.

6
Coves d'Artà

A fascinating network of underground caverns, whose weird stalactites and stalagmites conjure up mysterious images of Heaven and Hell.

If you only have time to visit one set of caves on the east coast, this is the one to see. Now that they are a sanitised

Back into daylight as you emerge from the caves

tourist attraction, it is hard to imagine how French geologist Édouard Martel felt when he first stepped into these caves, dark, mysterious and terrifying, in 1876. In fact they had been known about for centuries – Jaume I found 2,000 Arabs hiding here with their cattle during the Christian conquest and they were later used by hermits, pirates and smugglers – but it was Martel who first studied and chronicled these grottoes, 46m above the sea at Cap Vermell, at the instigation of Archduke Ludwig Salvator. Another early visitor was Jules Verne; the caves are said to have inspired his *Journey to the Centre of the Earth*.

The guided tour comes with special effects and the various chambers are given Dantesque names – Hell, Purgatory, Paradise. The descent into Hell is swiftly followed by a *son et lumière* display. Stalactites point down from the mouldy roof like daggers, somehow defying gravity. One of the chambers is as large as the nave of Palma Cathedral, and the Queen of Pillars, a stalagmite 22m tall, could almost be a Gothic column. It is growing upwards at the rate of 2cm every 100 years; in another 5,000 years or so it will be joined to the ceiling.

You emerge from the caves to a view of the sea, framed by the cavern entrance. Disabled visitors and others with limited mobility will find the staircases in here particularly difficult. All visitors should be sensibly shod, as the floor can be slippery.

 29F4

 841293

 Jul–Sep, daily 10–7; Oct–Jun, daily 10–5

 Bars at Platja de Canyamel near by (£)

 From Artà and Cala Rajada in summer

 None

 Moderate

7

Deià

An idyllic village of green-shuttered, ochre-coloured houses has become a millionaires' hideaway in the shadow of the Teix mountain.

28B4

Wide choice of restaurants and bars (£)

From Palma, Valldemossa and Port de Sóller

From Port de Sóller to Cala de Deià on Fri in summer

Lluc-Alcari (▶ 58), Son Marroig (▶ 88)

Classical music festival in Jul & Aug

Deià could have been just another pretty Mallorcan village had Robert Graves not decided to make it his home. The English poet and novelist first moved here in 1932 with his mistress Laura Riding and returned in 1946 with his second wife. Muses followed, friends came to stay, and before long Deià had established a reputation as a foreign artists' colony. Now it is on every tourist itinerary as the prime example of 'the other Mallorca' and this small village contains two luxury hotels. Rich foreign residents, like the actor Michael Douglas, are apt to bemoan the arrival of tour buses; the few locals who remain are philosophical about outsiders.

Graves was hardly the first to discover Deià. An 1878 guidebook noted its 'collection of strange and eccentric foreigners' and it has stayed that way ever since. Climb the Carrer es Puig, Deià's only real street, passing ceramic Stations of the Cross, to reach the parish church and the small cemetery where Graves is buried. His tombstone, like many others, is inscribed in simple handwriting set into the drying concrete – *Robert Graves, Poeta, 1895–1985*. If you want to know more, read *Wild Olives – Life in Majorca with Robert Graves* by his son William Graves.

From Deià you can scramble down to Cala de Deià, a small shingle beach set in an attractive cove, where local artists still continue the Graves tradition of naked swimming and long parties at weekends.

Deià is a lot more cosmopolitan than it looks

8
Lluc

*Mallorca's most sacred site –
a former monastery in a spectacular setting in the
Serra de Tramuntana.*

Lluc has been a centre of pilgrimage since the 13th century when an Arab shepherd boy, newly converted to Christianity, discovered a dark wooden statue of the Virgin in a cleft in the rock. The image was placed in the local church but three times it returned miraculously to its cave, whereupon the villagers recognised a message from God and built a chapel to house it.

La Moreneta ('the Little Dark One') is now encrusted with precious stones, and sits in a chapel decorated with the arms of every Mallorcan town. Pilgrims and tourists queue to pay homage, especially on Sundays and at 11AM before the daily concerts by Els Blauets choir. The choir, named after their blue cassocks, was established in 1531, comprising 40 boys, 'natives of Mallorca, of pure blood, sound in grammar and song'. The service is marred by the whirring and flashing of cameras, and if it's meditation you seek, come back instead for the evening Mass.

The monastery complex includes Els Porxerets, the former pilgrims' quarters with stabling beneath the rooms, and the Way of the Rosary, with touches by Antoni Gaudí. From the hilltop cross you look down over an unexpected farmland valley and up into the pine-covered mountains. You can stay at Lluc but it is more like a hotel than a hermitage – the 100 'cells' have *en suite* bathrooms and there are several restaurants and bars. There is also a **museum** – among the displays of ceramics, chalices and coins is a collection of paintings by the 20th-century Mallorcan artist Josep Coll Bardolet, with scenes from Deià, Valldemossa and Fornalutx.

The chapel at Lluc is dedicated to the Virgin Mary

✝ 28C5

☎ 517025

🕐 Daily 10–5:30

🍴 Choice of restaurants and bars – best restaurant (££) in the former monks' refectory

🚌 Two buses daily from Palma and Inca

✋ Monastery: free. Museum: cheap

❓ Choir concert daily 11:15 followed by Mass at 11:30; second service at dusk open to those staying; annual night-time pilgrimage from Palma to Lluc on foot (48km) – usually held in first week of Aug

9
La Seu (Palma Cathedral)

The glory of Palma – a magnificent Gothic cathedral whose sandstone walls and flying buttresses seem to rise out of the sea.

Anything you see inside Palma cathedral will come as a disappointment once you have stood on the seafront and gazed up at its golden sandstone exterior, climbing above the old city walls. La Seu stands out utterly from its surroundings, a demonstration of the might of Mallorca's Christian conquerors to all who arrived by sea.

Tradition has it that a storm arose as Jaume I was sailing towards Mallorca. He vowed that if he landed safely he would build a great church in honour of the Virgin. On New Year's Day 1230, a day after the fall of Palma, the foundation stone was symbolically laid on the site of the city's main mosque. Work continued for 400 years – and had to resume in 1851 when an earthquake destroyed the west front. More touches were added this century by the Catalan architect Antoni Gaudí.

You enter through a side door, passing a small museum; head for the west portal and gaze down the long nave. Light pours in through the rose window, one of the world's largest, 12m across and studded with 1,236 pieces of stained glass. The columns are ringed with wrought-iron candelabra by Gaudí; his most controversial addition is the unfinished Crown of Thorns, fashioned from cardboard and cork and suspended above the altar.

Be sure to walk around to the south front, facing the sea, to look at the Portal del Mirador, a 15th-century door by Guillem Sagrera featuring scenes from the Last Supper.

✚ 34B2

✉ Carrer Palau Reial 29

☎ 723130

🕐 Apr–Oct, Mon–Fri 10–6, Sat 10–2; Nov–Mar, Mon–Fri 10–3, Sat 10–2

♿ Few

✋ Cheap (free for services)

↔ Museu Diocesà (▶ 37), Palau de l'Almudaina (▶ 38)

❓ High Mass, Sun 10:30

Even the royal palace is cut down to size by the mystery of Palma cathedral, standing out above its surroundings on the waterfront

10
Valldemossa

28B4

Choice of restaurants and bars (££)

From Palma, Deià and Port de Sóller

Chopin piano concerts Mon–Sat 10:30, 11:30, 12:30 in Palau del Rei Sanç (entered on same ticket as monastery); La Beata procession in honour of Santa Catalina Thomás, 27–8 Jul; Chopin Festival in Aug; market held Sun

Reial Cartoixa

612106

Mon–Sat, 9:30–1, 3–5:30 (till 6:30 Apr–Sep)

Reial Cartoixa: expensive

The small town in the mountains where Mallorcan tourism began one cold, damp winter in 1838.

Try as it might – and it doesn't try very hard – Valldemossa cannot escape its connection with Frédéric Chopin and his lover George Sand. They arrived in 1838, having rented a former monk's cell, planning to carry on their affair away from the gossip of Paris and hoping that the climate would benefit Chopin's health (he had tuberculosis). Nothing worked out as planned. The weather was wet and windy, the couple were shunned by the locals, Chopin's piano failed to arrive and the relationship never recovered. Sand took out her anger on Valldemossa in a spiteful book, *Winter in Majorca*, which the locals, labelled as thieves and savages, still gleefully sell to visitors.

The **Reial Cartoixa** (Royal Carthusian Monastery) is the focus of any visit – white-arched corridors lead to 'cells' containing museums on various themes. Visit the old pharmacy – you can almost smell the herbs – then look into the library, where the monks would meet for half an hour a week, their only human contact. There is a fine modern art museum, with works by Picasso, Miró and Juli Ramis, and of course there is Chopin's cell...

Most people come for the Chopin experience, but there is more to Valldemossa than that. It is also the birthplace of Catalina Thomás, Mallorca's patron saint. A peasant girl born in 1531, she became a nun in Palma and was renowned for her humility. She died in 1574, was beatified in 1792 and achieved sainthood in 1935. Almost every home in Valldemossa has a plaque imploring her prayers, and her birthplace at Carrer Rectoría 5 has been turned into a shrine. She would probably be appalled.

The Carthusian monastery stands at the centre of the highest town in Mallorca

What To See

27

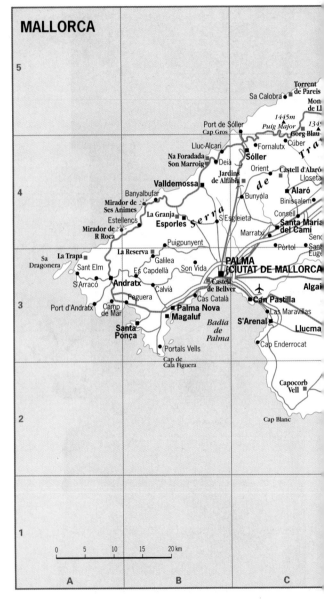

MALLORCA

Torrent
de Pareis

Sa Calobra

Mon
de Ll

Port de Sóller
Cap Gros

1445m
Puig Major   *134*
Gorg Blau

Cúber

Tra

Lluc-Alcari

Fornalutx

Na Foradada
Son Marroig

Deià   **Sóller**

Orient   Castell d'Alaró

Lloseta

Valldemossa

Jardins
de Alfàbia

de

Alaró

Banyalbufar

Bunyola

Binissalem

Mirador de
Ses Animes

La Granja

Consell

Estellencs

S'Esgleieta

**Santa María
del Camí**

Mirador de
R Roca

Esporles

Serra

Marratxí

Sen

Pòrtol   Sant
Euge

Sa
Dragonera

La Trapa

La Reserva

Puigpunyent

Galilea

Es Capdellà

Sant Elm

Son Vida

**PALMA
CIUTAT DE MALLORCA**

S'Arracó

Andratx

Calvià

Algai

Port d'Andratx

Peguera

Camp
de Mar

Cas Català

Castell
de Bellver

Can Pastilla

Las Maravillas

Palma Nova
Magaluf

*Badia
de
Palma*

S'Arenal

Llucma

**Santa
Ponça**

Portals Vells

Cap de
Cala Figuera

Cap Enderrocat

Capocorb
Vell

Cap Blanc

0   5   10   15   20 km

A   B   C

5

4

3

2

1

Cap de Formentor

Mirador des Colomer

Cala Sant Vicenç

Formentor

Castell del Rei

Port de Pollença

Cap des Pinar

Pollença

Badia de Pollença

Puig de Maria

Ermita de la Victoria

Alcúdia

Port d'Alcúdia

ana

Coves de Campanet

Badia d'Alcúdia

Cap de Ferrutx

Platja de Murro

S'Albufera

Can Picafort

Sa Pobla

Ermita de Betlem

Cap des Freu

Muro

Colònia de Sant Pere

Cala Rajada

Ermita de Santa Magdalena

ca

Santa Margalida

Punta de Capdepera

Llubí

Artà

Capdepera

Sineu

Maria de la Salut

Ses Païsses

Coves d'Artà

Cap Vermell

Son Servera

Sa Costa des Pins

Pina

Sant Joan

Petra

Sant Llorenç des Cardassar

Cala Bona

Ermita de Bonany

Auto-Safari

Cala Millor

Montuïri

Vilafranca de Bonany

Sa Coma

Punta de n'Amer

Serra de Llevant

Manacor

Coves dels Hams

uari de Cura
543m
Puig de Randa
la

Porreres

Porto Cristo

Coves del Drac

Felanitx

509m
Puig de Sant Salvador

Santuari de Sant Salvador

Porto Colom

issa

Campos

Castell de Santueri

Sa Ràpita

Cala d'Or

Ses Covetes

Santanyí

Porto Petro

Platja
s Trenc

Ses Salines

Cala Mondragó

Colònia de Sant Jordi

Botanicáctus

Cala Figuera

Cala Santanyí

Cala Llombards

Cap de Ses Salines

Sa Conillera

Cabrera

| D | E | F |

Palma

Palma comes as a surprise to many people – it is stylish, sophisticated, intimate yet bursting with life. Half of Mallorca's population live here, enjoying the island's best restaurants, shops and nightlife as well as a thriving arts scene and a lively café society.

Palma's masterpiece is its Gothic cathedral, rising out of the city walls which once marked the edge of the sea. Close to here is the old Arab quarter, its maze of narrow streets hiding museums, palaces and exquisite courtyards. But do not explore old Palma at the expense of its modern side. Take coffee in the former Gran Hotel, visit an art gallery in a converted mansion, join Palma's bright young things on their evening *passeig* along the waterfront, and you will begin to appreciate the variety of this fascinating city.

'The time will doubtless come when frail dilettantes, and even lovely women, will be able to visit Palma with no more exhaustion and discomfort than Geneva.'

GEORGE SAND
Winter in Majorca (1855), translated
by Robert Graves (1956)

Palma

Known to the Arabs as Medina Mayurqa and to Mallorcans simply as *Ciutat* (City), Palma is in fact named after the Roman city of Palmaria. Here you can almost literally uncover the different layers of Mallorcan history. The Roman city still exists, a metre or two beneath the ground; inhabitants of houses near the cathedral are still discovering Roman remains. The cathedral was built on the site of a mosque, once a Roman temple; the royal palace replaced an Arab *alcázar*.

The city you see today, however, is a relatively recent creation. The tree-lined promenades of La Rambla and Passeig des Born, home to florists and newspaper sellers, were built in the 19th century on a dried-up river bed. The walls which once surrounded the city were pulled down to create the ring road Las Avingudas, and Passeig Marítim, the waterfront highway and promenade, was only reclaimed from the sea in the 1950s.

Most of the main sights are located within the area bounded by the old walls, especially to the north and east of the cathedral. Wander along any alley in the ancient Arab quarter, peering through wrought-iron gates and heavy wooden doors, and you will be rewarded with glimpses of one magnificent patio after another, with their stone staircases, galleries and arcades.

But you have not truly seen Palma until you have surveyed it from the waterfront, with the cathedral and Almudaina palace rising proudly above the defensive walls of the old city, their golden sandstone lit up by the afternoon sun.

Palma's pedestrian shopping streets seem designed for browsing – but everything stops during the afternoon siesta

What to See in Palma

BANYS ÀRABS (ARAB BATHS) ✪✪

These 10th-century baths are virtually all that remain of the Arab city of Medina Mayurqa. They were probably part of a nobleman's house and are similar to those found in other Islamic cities. The *tepidarium* has a dome in the shape of a half-orange, with 25 round shafts for sunlight, supported by a dozen columns. Notice how each of the columns is different – they were probably salvaged from the ruins of various Roman buildings, an early example of recycling. *Hammams* were meeting-places as well as wash-houses, and the courtyard with its cactus, palm and orange trees would have made a pleasant place to cool off after a hot bath.

BASÍLICA DE SANT FRANCESC ✪✪

The façade of this 13th-century church (remodelled after it was struck by lightning in the 17th century) is typically Mallorcan – a massive, forbidding sandstone wall with a delicately carved portal and a rose window at the centre. You enter through peaceful Gothic cloisters with orange and lemon trees and a well at the centre. Inside the church is the tomb of Ramón Llull (1235–1316), the Catalan mystic who became a hermit following a failed seduction attempt and was later stoned to death attempting to convert Muslims in Tunisia. His statue can be seen on the Palma seafront; outside the basilica is a statue of another famous Mallorcan missionary, Fray Junípero Serra, who once lived in the monastery here. The streets behind the church, once home to jewellers and Jewish traders, are now run-down and seedy and best avoided after dark.

CASTELL DE BELLVER
(▶ 20, TOP TEN)

An impressive baroque portal gives relief to the stern façade of Palma's mighty Basílica de Sant Francesc

---

 35C1
 Carrer Can Serra 7
 721549
 Apr–Oct, daily 9:30–7;
Nov–Mar, daily 9:30–6
Bar Sa Murada near by (£)
None
Cheap
Museu de Mallorca
(▶ 37)

35C2
Plaça Sant Francesc
712695
Mon–Sat 9:30–1, 3:30–6,
Sun 9:30–1
 Cheap

COLLECCIÓ MARCH

This small collection of 20th-century Spanish art belonged to the Mallorcan banker Joan March, once one of the world's richest men. There are just 36 pieces, each by a different artist, including Picasso, Dali and Miró. Some of the exhibits are the sort of thing that give modern art a bad name, but do go with an open mind.

35C3
Carrer Sant Miquel 11
713515
Mon–Fri 10–6:30, Sat 10–1:30
Cafés in Plaça Major (£)
None Cheap

FUNDACIÓ LA CAIXA

The Gran Hotel was Palma's first luxury hotel when it opened in 1903. Designed by the Catalan architect Lluís Domènech i Montaner, it was the building which began the craze for modernista (art nouveau) architecture in the city. Restored by the Fundació la Caixa and reopened in 1993, it is now an art gallery featuring changing exhibitions and a permanent display of paintings by Hermen Anglada-Camarasa, the founder of the 'Pollença school'. On the ground floor there is a bookshop and a trendy café-bar.

35C3
Plaça Weyler 3
720111
Tue–Sat 10–9, Sun 10–2
Café and restaurant (££)
Good
Free

LA LLOTJA

With twin turrets and an angel over the door, this 15th-century seafront building looks half-castle, half-church. In fact it is neither. It was designed by Guillem Sagrera (the architect of the cathedral's Portal del Mirador) as the city's exchange. Stand among the spiralling pillars, gaze up at the rib vaulting, and try to imagine the merchants of 500 years ago haggling over silk, spices and silver. Nowadays La Llotja is a cultural centre, hosting temporary exhibitions.

34A2
Plaça Llotja
711705
Tue–Sat 11–2, 5–9, Sun 11–2
Wide choice of restaurants and bars near by (£–££)
Good
Free

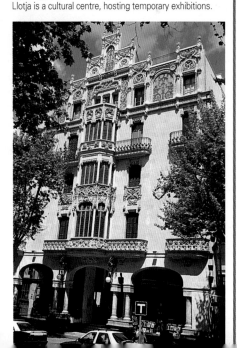

Modern art, inside and out, at Fundació la Caixa – the 'in' place to meet for coffee and cakes

33

PALMA CITY CENTRE

0   250   500 m

The map contains the following labels:

COMTE DE SALLENT · BLANQUERNA · 31 DE DICIEMBRE · ARXIDUC LLUIS SALVADOR · EUSEBIO · PLAÇA CONQUISTA · AV. JUAN MARCH · Ferrocarriles de Mallorca · Hospital Militar · SANT MIQUEL · PLAÇA D'ESPANYA · Estació de autobúses · Santa Catalina · AVINGUDA · anta Magdalena · Santa Magdalena · RAMBLA · PLAÇA DEL OLIVAR · Mercat Olivar · ALEXANDRE · ROSSELLÓ · Col·lecció March · Sant Miquel · La Mercet · SINDICAT · dació aixa / n Hotel · Teatre Principal · PLAÇA MAJOR · PLAÇA WEYLER · PLAÇA DE SANT ANTONIO · GA L CAT · Palau de Justícia · VILLALONGA · Santa Eulàlia · Palau Vivot · PLAÇA CORT · PLAÇA SANTA EULALIA · PLAÇA QUADRADO · ntament · PLAÇA SANT FRANCESC · Basílica de Sant Francesc · Socorro · ALOMAR · Arc de lmudaina · seu cesà · Museu de Mallorca · El Temple · Banys Àrabs · Montesió · San Jerónimo · Santa Clara · Parc de la Mar · AVINGUDA DE GABRIEL · JOAN MARAGALL · C · D

Mallorcan street art – a performance artist turns into a statue at the foot of Passeig de la Rambla

A Walk Around Palma

Distance
3.5km

Time
2 hours plus coffees,
browsing and visits – probably
half a day

Start/end point
Plaça d'Espanya
✚ 35D4
🚌 Most city and island-wide
buses terminate here
🚆 Trains from Inca and
Sóller also terminate here

Lunch
Fundació la Caixa (££)
✉ Plaça Weyler 3
☎ 728077

This walk starts in Plaça d'Espanya and passes close to all of Palma's main sights. Begin by heading for Mercat Olivar (▶ 37), where you can look round the market.

Leave via Plaça Olivar and turn left into Carrer Sant Miquel.

Soon you reach Plaça Major with its outdoor cafés and street entertainers.

Continue across the square; fork right into Carrer Jaume II.

At the end of this pedestrian shopping street, don't fail to look up at the *modernista* façade of Sa Nostra bank before turning left into Plaça Cort. Beyond a gnarled olive tree you see the town hall.

Take the short street to the left of the town hall to reach Plaça Santa Eulàlia; cross this square diagonally and take Carrer Morey.

This brings you into the heart of the old city. Take your time here admiring the courtyards; don't miss Casa Oleza at No 9.

Continue straight on to Carrer Miramar and turn right onto the city walls.

The cathedral (▶ 24–5) is above you; to visit it and the palace, climb the steps to a large wooden cross.

Plaça Major – a good place to stop for a coffee. There is a craft market held here on summer mornings

Back on the walls, continue until you drop to the S'Hort del Rei gardens (▶ 38). Cross Plaça Reina and walk up the Born (▶ 39), turning right by Bar Bosch into Carrer Unió.

Look out for the old Gran Hotel (▶ 33) on your left and the bakery opposite, two good examples of *modernista* style. Beyond the theatre, the road bends left and becomes La Rambla; stroll up this promenade among the flower stalls.

At the top of La Rambla, turn right into Carrer Oms and follow it back to Plaça d'Espanya.

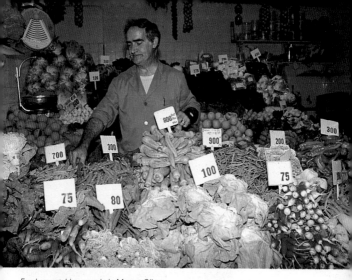

Fresh vegetables on sale in Mercat Olivar

MERCAT OLIVAR ✪✪

When you're tired of tourist sights and want to meet the people of Palma instead, head for this covered market. It is a feast for the eyes – dazzling displays of flowers, huge piles of oranges, buckets full of olives, fish you never knew existed. Those of a squeamish disposition should avoid the upstairs meat counters, where the pigs and rabbits look like pigs and rabbits rather than sterile pieces of packaged flesh. A good place to buy ham and cheese, or to stop for *tortilla* at one of the *tapas* stalls, where the workers drink brandy with their breakfast coffee.

➕ 35D4
✉ Plaça Olivar
☎ 724650
🕐 Mon–Sat 7–2
🍴 Several *tapas* bars (£) upstairs
♿ Free

MUSEU DIOCESÀ ✪

This small museum of religious and historical artefacts is based in a wing of the former episcopal palace tucked behind the cathedral. Among the paintings, pulpits and prayer books are splendid Arab tapestries, a collection of ceramics spanning five centuries and a 17th-century painting of baby Jesus carrying a cross. Look out for the portrait of St George (Sant Jordi) with medieval Palma in the background.

➕ 35C2
✉ Carrer Mirador 5
☎ 714063
🕐 Apr–Oct, Mon–Fri 10–1:30, 3–8, Sat–Sun 10–1:30; Nov–Mar, Mon–Fri 10–1:30, 3–6, Sat–Sun 10–1:30
♿ Cheap
🔁 La Seu (► 24)

MUSEU DE MALLORCA ✪

Billed as Mallorca's most important museum, this undoubtedly contains some fascinating exhibits but the displays lack imagination and it is difficult to get excited about bits of stone in glass cases if you do not understand the captions. Talaiotic and Roman remains are followed by Moorish ceramics and Christian art, providing a quick overview of Mallorcan history. It's worth the entrance fee just to see the building, a 17th-century palace built on the foundations of one of Mallorca's earliest Arab houses.

➕ 35C2
✉ Carrer Portella 5
☎ 717540
🕐 Tue–Sat 10–2, 4–7, Sun 10–2
🍴 Bar Sa Murada (£) at foot of Carrer Portella
♿ Cheap
🔁 Banys Àrabs (► 32)

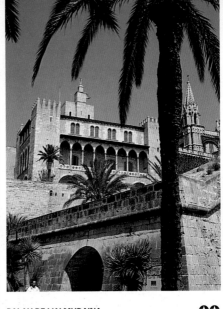

Palma's royal palace was built as a Muslim fortress and still has a very Islamic feel to it

---

<table>
<tr><td>➕</td><td>34B2</td></tr>
<tr><td>✉</td><td>Carrer Palau Reial</td></tr>
<tr><td>☎</td><td>727145</td></tr>
<tr><td>🕐</td><td>Palace: Apr–Sep, Mon–Fri 10–6:30, Sat 10–2; Oct–Mar, Mon–Fri 10–2, 4–6, Sat 10–2; Gardens: open access</td></tr>
<tr><td>♿</td><td>Wheelchair access on request</td></tr>
<tr><td>💶</td><td>Palace: moderate; Gardens: free</td></tr>
<tr><td>🔗</td><td>La Seu (▶ 24–5)</td></tr>
<tr><td>❓</td><td>Still used by King Juan Carlos for official functions in Palma</td></tr>
</table>

PALAU DE L'ALMUDAINA ✪✪

A royal palace has stood on this site since the Muslim *walis* (governors) built their *alcázar* soon after the Arab conquest. It was converted into Gothic style under Jaume II, but elements of Islamic architecture remain – like the Moorish arches seen from the seafront, lit up at night like a row of lanterns. The courtyard, laid out in 1309 and flanked by palm trees, is at its best in late afternoon when the sun falls on the cathedral towers overhead. Just off the courtyard is the royal chapel, Capella de Santa Ana.

The S'Hort del Rei gardens beneath the palace make a pleasant place to sit beneath the fountains watching the world go by. Look out for the Arc de la Drassana, once the gateway to the royal docks; near here is a statue of a *hondero* or Balearic slinger. The gardens were rebuilt in the 1960s, forcing the demolition of several houses; their best-known landmark is Joan Miró's *Egg* sculpture, which few people can resist sticking their heads through.

<table>
<tr><td>➕</td><td>35C1</td></tr>
<tr><td>🍴</td><td>Choice of cafés (£)</td></tr>
<tr><td>💶</td><td>Free</td></tr>
<tr><td>❓</td><td>Free concerts summer evenings and Sun lunchtimes</td></tr>
</table>

PARC DE LA MAR ✪✪

Until the 1960s the sea reached up to the city walls, providing the perfect reflection for the cathedral. When the building of a new road changed all that, an artificial lake was constructed to reproduce the effect. The park around the lake is now a popular weekend and summer spot, with several cafés, outdoor concerts, a mural donated by Joan Miró and an art gallery in the vaults of the old city walls. Sit beneath the palm trees gazing up at the cathedral and try to imagine the travellers of days gone by arriving at this same spot from the sea by boat.

PASSEIG DES BORN

○○

For more than a century this short, tree-lined promenade has been at the heart of city life; it has witnessed *festas*, demonstrations and countless generations of families enjoying an evening stroll. During the Franco era it was renamed after the dictator, but everyone still called it 'the Born'. Come here to take the pulse of Palma from a seat at a pavement café – Bar Bosch, near the top of the Born in Plaça Rei Joan Carles I, is the traditional place. Near here is **Ca'n Solleric**, a modern art gallery which opened in 1995 in a converted mansion.

✚ 34B3
🍴 Wide choice of restaurants and cafés near by (£–££)

Ca'n Solleric
✉ Passeig des Born 27
☎ 722092
🕐 Tue–Sat 10:30–1:45, 5–8:30, Sun 10–1:45
✋ Free

POBLE ESPANYOL (SPANISH VILLAGE)

○

Spain gets the theme-park treatment at this 'village' in the outskirts of Palma, where reproductions of famous buildings from Córdoba, Toledo and Madrid are gathered together with typical houses from the Spanish regions. You can eat Spanish food in the Plaza Mayor (Spanish spellings here) or sit outside a café watching the tourists buy pearls and souvenirs at the village shops. A visit here gives you a whistle-stop tour of Spanish architecture, showing its development through Muslim and then Christian influences. If you have never been to Granada, it's worth coming just for the reproduction of the salon, baths and patio from the Alhambra Palace. Various artists give displays of handicrafts in workshops scattered throughout the 'village'.

✚ 72B2
✉ Carrer Poble Espanyol 39
☎ 737075
🕐 Apr–Oct, daily 9–8; Nov–Mar, daily 9–6
🍴 Restaurant and cafés (££)
🚌 5
✋ Moderate
❓ Craft displays from 10 to one hour before closing time

LA SEU (▶ 24–5, TOP TEN)

'The Born' once hosted jousting contests but now the biggest battle is for a seat at a pavement café

A Walk by the Sea

Distance
3km one way

Time
1½ hours

Start point
Passeig Sagrera
🚇 34A2
🚌 1, 4, 15, 21

End point
Club de Mar
🚌 1

Lunch
Taberna de la Boveda (££)
✉ Passeig Sagrera 3
☎ 720026

This walk along Palma's waterfront is good in the early morning, as the city stirs itself and the fish market comes to life; or late in the day as the sun sets over the sea, the pavement bars begin to buzz and the cathedral and castle light up for the night.

Start in Passeig Sagrera, at the foot of Avinguda d'Antoni Maura by the statue of Ramón Llull.

This short tree-lined avenue, named after the architect of La Llotja, passes several interesting buildings. First, La Llotja itself (▶ 33), Palma's masterpiece of Gothic civic architecture; Porta Vella del Moll, the old gateway to the city from the sea; and finally Consulat del Mar, the former maritime court which houses the Balearic government.

At the end of Passeig Sagrera, cross the main road to reach the fishing port, marked by lines of blue nets.

West of here, in a small garden, is the oratory of Sant Elm, designed as a navigators' chapel, later used as a tavern, and moved here stone by stone from Passeig Sagrera in 1947.

From here the walk is straightforward – just follow the seafront west along Passeig Marítim, using the promenade between the road and the sea. A cycle path, also used by joggers, runs alongside the promenade.

Pass Reial Club Nautic, facing a section of city wall and a row of windmills; look up ahead to see Bellver Castle on its hill. As you walk on, turn around to look back at the cathedral, seen across the bay through a forest of masts. From a jetty opposite the Auditorium theatre, excursion boats offer tours of Palma Bay. Keep going, and eventually you reach Club de Mar with its luxury yachts. Just beyond here is the commercial ferry port, where boats leave for Barcelona, Valencia, Menorca and Ibiza.

Return the same way, or take bus 1 back to Passeig Sagrera.

Around the Island

Each region of Mallorca has its own particular appeal – the northeast for history, the east coast for beaches and caves, the north and west for spectacular mountains and picture-postcard villages. And you haven't seen Mallorca until you have driven across *es pla*, the fertile plain at the centre of the island, with its almond groves, windmills and old market towns.

Try to do a bit of everything – one monastery, one mountain walk, one quiet cove – but don't try to do too much. The twisting mountain roads get very crowded in summer and journeys take longer than you think. Take your time and avoid the worst of the heat by doing what the Mallorcans do, break for a siesta. It is generally far more rewarding to spend a day pottering around one small area than to hare from one town to another ticking off the sights.

---

*' If you would experience
the most perfect method of
travelling, ride upon a mule,
under a Mediterranean sun,
along a golden road that
leads down from the
mountains to the sea. '*

GORDON WEST
Jogging Round Majorca (1929)

What to See Around the Island

ALCÚDIA (► 16, TOP TEN)

ALGAIDA ✪

Algaida is a typical Mallorcan town, all green shutters, narrow streets without pavements and a central square dominated by a sandstone church. Few visitors make it into the town centre; the attractions are all on the outskirts, on the Palma–Manacor road. The main one is **Ca'n Gordiola**, a glass factory housed in a mock castle. The ground floor contains a workshop (though it looks more like a church with its arches and stained glass) where you can watch glass being blown; upstairs there are museums devoted to both glass and perfume. A further 2km along the road to Manacor is a string of well-known restaurants, where the people of Palma head at weekends for old-fashioned Mallorcan cuisine.

ANDRATX ✪

Like many towns around the coast, Andratx was built several kilometres inland from its port in a bid to deter pirate raids. In the late 20th century the town is reaping an unexpected benefit – tourists pour into the port, spending money which the town collects in taxes, yet except on market day Andratx sees little of the visitors and its people are left to get on with their lives. Surrounded by orange groves, and almond trees which leave a 'snowfall' of blossom each February, Andratx is a sleepy town which only really gets animated on Wednesdays when the streets are taken over by market stalls selling vegetables, cheeses and fish. When you have finished your shopping, climb to the top of the town to see the 13th-century church of Santa Maria.

🔸 28C3
🍴 Restaurants on the Palma–Manacor road (££)
🚌 From Palma
↔ Puig de Randa (► 75)
❓ Market held Fri

Ca'n Gordiola
✉ Carretera Palma–Manacor, km19
☎ 665046
🕐 Apr–Oct, Mon–Sat 9–8, Sun 9–1:30; Nov–Mar, Mon–Sat 9–1:30, 3–7:30, Sun 9–1:30
✋ Free

🔸 28A3
🍴 Bars and cafés (£)
🚌 Regular buses from Palma, Peguera and Port d'Andratx
↔ Port d'Andratx (► 67), Sant Elm (► 79)
❓ Market held Wed

Almonds from the orchards around Andratx are one of the bargains you can pick up in the weekly market

The West

Distance
62km

Time
3–4 hours plus lunch and time
at La Granja

Start/end point
Andratx
➕ 28A3

Lunch
La Granja (£)
☎ 610032

This drive gives an excellent introduction to the mountain and coastal scenery of western Mallorca.

Start in Andratx, taking the C710 to Estellencs about halfway up the main street.

Immediately the road begins to climb. You pass a *mirador* sign, go through a tunnel and the sea comes into view. Follow this beautiful twisting coast road between the sea and the pine-scented hills to the village of Estellencs, one of the prettiest in Mallorca, with narrow, steep cobbled streets and women doing their washing at the village well. After another 5km, stop at the Mirador de Ses Animes and clamber up to the 16th-century watchtower for views right along the northwest coast. Soon after this you reach Banyalbufar (► 46), with its spectacular terracing.

When the C710 turns off left towards Valldemossa, keep straight on the PM110, signposted to Palma. After 1km you see a sign to La Granja on your right.

You pass several coastal watchtowers, including this one near the village of Estellencs

You could easily spend 2–3 hours at this display of Mallorcan traditions (► 57).

Leaving La Granja, take the narrow road to Puigpunyent from the car park.

Follow this road for 10km, a dramatic journey through olive groves in the shadow of Puig de Galatzó. The road continues through Puigpunyent and on to Galilea (► 56), a mountain village with a couple of *tapas* bars and views out to sea. From here the road twists and turns down to the village of Es Capdella.

Turn right in the village and follow signs back to Andratx.

A flight of steps leads to Artà's hilltop sanctuary

ARTÀ ✪✪

Derived from the Arabic word *jertan* ('garden'), Artà has been occupied for at least 3,000 years, as evidenced by the remains of a Bronze Age site at Ses Païsses (▶85) just outside the town. Nowadays Artà is a prosperous little town near the coast, which gets particularly lively each Tuesday on market day.

From the parish church of Transfiguració del Senyor, an avenue of cypress trees leads to Artà's crowning glory, its hilltop fortress and Santuari de Sant Salvador. The view down over the rooftops, a jumble of tiles in every shade of brown, is one of the sights of Mallorca. On the site of a Moorish fortress, the original sanctuary walls and chapel were rebuilt in the 19th centrury. Walk around the battlements, rest in a peaceful courtyard, then look into the sanctuary church with its vivid paintings of two Mallorcan heroes – Jaume the Conqueror receiving the surrender of the *walis*, and Ramón Llull being stoned to death in Tunisia. There is also a painting of Sant Antoni, patron saint of Artà and of animals, seen here as always, with a small pig. Each January the saint is commemorated with a masked procession and a blessing of pets. Artà's big festival, Sant Antoni de Juny, dates back to 1581 and features dancers with cardboard horses strapped to their hips.

Artà's small **museum**, housed inside Sa Nostra bank, has archaeological discoveries from Greek and Roman periods.

🟥 29E4
🍴 Several bars and restaurants (£–££)
🚌 From Palma and Cala Rajada
↔ Ses Païsses (▶85)
❓ Market held Tue; Sant Antoni Abat, procession and blessing of pets, 16–17 Jan; Sant Antoni de Juny, *cavallets* horse dances, 13 Jun

Museum
✉ Carrer Estrella 4
☎ 835505
🕐 Mon–Fri 10–12
🎫 Free

AUTO-SAFARI ✪

Mallorca's only zoo consists of a 4-km drive through open countryside, passing giraffes, zebra, flamingos and deer (keep your car windows shut against marauding monkeys), followed by a 'baby zoo' with elephants, crocodiles and various young animals. You can also explore the 44-hectare reserve by a special 'mini-train' for which you pay a hefty supplement on top of the already considerable cost of entry.

🟥 29F3
✉ Carretera Porto Cristo–Son Servera, km5
☎ 810909
🕐 Apr–Sep, daily 9–7; Nov–Mar, daily 9–5
🍴 Café (£)
♿ Good
🎫 Expensive

The terraced slopes of Banyalbufar, created over a thousand years, reach right down to the sea

BANYALBUFAR ✪✪

People come to Banyalbufar to see one thing – its terraced hillsides, sloping down to the sea. Developed by the Moors and divided by drystone walls, these terraces speak powerfully of man's ingenuity in creating farmland out of inhospitable cliffs. Until recently it was the custom for each generation to add a further tier. In Moorish times the town, whose Arabic name means 'vineyard by the sea', was famed for its Malvasia wine – nowadays the terraces are mostly used to grow vegetables, though a few vines have been planted once again. Banyalbufar's popularity with foreign artists has led some people to conclude that it will be the next Deià (► 22).

BINISSALEM ✪

If you order Mallorcan wine in a restaurant, it will probably come from Binissalem. Viticulture was introduced here by the Romans and has survived in much reduced form. The reputation of Binissalem red wines, made with the local grape Manto Negro, has been growing in recent years – the best-known *bodega*, José L Ferrer, is on the right as you enter the town from Palma. If you are buying, remember *crianza* is good, *reserva* even better, *gran reserva* the best.

CABRERA ✪

'Goat island' is the largest in a rocky archipelago lying 20km off the south coast. Pliny claimed it as the birthplace of Hannibal; during the Napoleonic Wars it became a notorious prison camp. Since 1916 it has been a military base and since 1991 a protected national park as well. You can only get there on a day trip by boat, with time to walk up to the 14th-century castle above the harbour and look out for seabirds nesting on the craggy cliffs.

CALA D'OR ✪✪

Each of the various *calas* (bays) along the east coast has its own distinctive character; in the case of Cala d'Or the word is 'chic'. Former fishing harbours have been turned into marinas; people come here to sail and dive, and drink champagne at waterfront bars. The villas are white and flat-roofed, in Ibizan style, designed in the 1930s by Pep Costa Ferrer, and the effect is surprisingly attractive. Nowadays Cala d'Or is the collective name for a string of resorts, beaches and coves; they include Porto Petro, around a horseshoe bay 2km to the south, and Cala Mondragó, a further 4km south, where a pair of sandy beaches are linked by a concrete path.

☩ 29E2
🍴 Wide choice of restaurants (££–£££)
🚌 From Palma

CALA FIGUERA ✪✪

More than anywhere else in Mallorca, Cala Figuera retains the atmosphere of a working fishing port. White-painted houses reach down to the water's edge and fishermen sit on the steps mending nets. If you get here early enough in the morning you might even see the catch coming in. A path follows around the tiny harbour and onto the cliffs, offering good views back towards the bay. The nearest beach is 4km to the south at Cala Santanyí.

☩ 29E2
🍴 Several seafood restaurants and others (££)
🚌 From Palma and Santanyí
↔ Santanyí (► 82)

CALA MAJOR ✪

Cala Major and its neighbour Sant Agusti were two of Mallorca's earliest resorts; now they are virtually suburbs of Palma. The tourists have moved elsewhere and there is a definite feel of an area that has seen better days. The king still comes, though, to his summer residence Marivent, where frequent guests include Britain's Prince Charles; and Mallorca's most important art collection is here, in Joan Miró's old house and studio (► 56).

☩ 72B2
🍴 Wide choice of restaurants (££)
🚌 3 from Palma
↔ Fundació Pilar i Joan Miró (► 56)

Fishermen's cottages at Cala Figuera

CALA MILLOR ✪

Fifty years ago this was a lonely dune-covered shore; now it has become the major resort on Mallorca's east coast. The main attraction is its fine sandy beaches; from Cala Bona ('the good bay') to Cala Millor ('the better bay') they stretch unbroken for 2km. In summer it is 'lively', travel-agent speak for brash, and best avoided unless you like discos and late-night bars; in winter it takes on a new atmosphere, as a resort for the 'young at heart', another travel-agent euphemism. To see what this coast used to be like, walk to the headland at Punta de n'Amer (▶ 76).

🔲 29F3
🍴 Wide choice of bars and restaurants (£–££)
🚌 From Palma; also from Cala Rajada and Port d'Alcúdia in summer
↔ Punta de n'Amer (▶ 76)

Cala Millor – the golden sands just go on and on

CALA RAJADA ✪

This fishing port on Mallorca's eastern tip, surrounded by fine beaches and pretty coves, has two different characters depending on when you go. In winter it virtually shuts down, apart from a few permanent locals and a handful of bars on the promenade; in summer it is a crowded resort, with windsurfing, snorkelling, and numerous discos. Many Germans have second homes here; there have been complaints in the Mallorcan press that it is becoming a 'German colony'.

A short walk uphill from the beach leads through woodland to the lighthouse at Punta de Capdepera. Also above the harbour are the Jardins Casa March, owned by the same banking family as the Collecció March in Palma. The gardens contain a sculpture park with works by Rodin, Henry Moore and modern Catalan artists. They can only be visited by prior arrangement with the tourist office.

🔲 29F4
🍴 Wide choice of restaurants (££)
🚌 From Palma and Porto Cristo; also from Cala Millor in summer
ℹ Tourist office: Plaça dels Pins (☎ 563033)
↔ Capdepera (▶ 50)
❓ Market held Sat; processions of boats, 16 Jul and 16 Aug; summer festival of evening concerts in Jardins Casa March

CALVIÀ ✪

Calvià is like an old lady who has won the *lotería* and doesn't know how to cope with her success. Until recently an unassuming country town, Calvià hit the jackpot when tourists discovered the nearby beaches and it is now said to be the richest municipality in Spain. There are a few ostentatious signs of wealth, like the sparkling new town

🔲 28B3
🍴 Choice of restaurants and bars (££)
🚌 20 from Palma
❓ Market held Mon

Tales of old Calvià in this ceramic display, created by local arts students to introduce visitors to the history of their town

hall and sports stadium, but mostly life continues as before, with ochre-coloured houses, a handful of shops and bars, and chickens scrambling between the olive trees. The town is dominated by the church of Sant Joan Baptista, built in the late 19th century around the 13th-century original; near here, by a fountain, a ceramic mural tells the story of Calvià's history. Founded in 1249 with 80 inhabitants, the town had a population of 3,000 in 1960 and 11,560 in 1980 – all because of tourism. Stand on the terrace looking out over almond and carob trees and it is hard to believe you are just a few kilometres from the teeming resorts of 'Maganova'.

CAMPOS ✪

Midway from Llucmajor to Santanyí on the C717, Campos was founded by Jaume II in 1300 on the site of earlier Roman and Arab settlements. A painting of Christ by the Sevillian artist Murillo hangs in the parish church of Sant Julià. Next door to the church is a museum with a large collection of offertory bowls. To visit both the church and the museum, collect the keys from the Casa Rectoría – follow the signs.

Campos has a busy market on Thursdays and Saturdays and its port adjoins the resort of Colònia de Sant Jordi (▶ 51) to the south.

✚ 29D2
🍴 Several cafés and bars (£)
🚌 From Palma
❓ Market held Thu, Sat

CAP DE FORMENTOR (► 18, TOP TEN)

CAPDEPERA ★★

If you are driving between Artà and Cala Rajada, stop off to visit this small town, crowned by the largest fortress in Mallorca. The Romans were the first to build a **castle** on this site – the Moors enlarged it, the Christians destroyed it, then replaced it with one of their own in the 14th century. Legend has it that the citizens of Cápdepera hid in the castle when under siege, placing an image of Our Lady of Hope on the battlements, and the invaders were driven away by fog. The miracle is recorded inside the castle in the Capella de Nostra Senyora de la Esperança and remembered each year at the town's annual *festa*. You reach the castle by climbing the steps from the market square, Plaça de l'Orient.

CAPOCORB VELL ★★

These are the most significant remains of the Talaiotic culture, which flourished in Mallorca between around 1300 and 800 BC. Villages were dominated by *talaiots*, circular or rectangular structures two to three storeys high, which were used as both burial chambers and defensive forts. Each settlement was surrounded by Cyclopean walls, built from massive, unhewn stones without mortar to hold them together. There is no evidence of a written language, so the stones are all that archaeologists have to go on in understanding prehistoric Mallorcan culture. At Capocorb Vell, 12km south of Llucmajor, you can see five *talaiots* and wander around the ancient village, 100m above sea level just inland from the coast. The Talaiotic people kept sheep, and the sound of sheep bells in the nearby fields is a touching reminder of continuity.

🗺 29F4

🍴 Café de l'Orient, Plaça de l'Orient (£)

🚌 From Palma and Cala Rajada

🔄 Cala Rajada (► 48)

❓ Market held Wed; Nostra Senyora de la Esperança *festa*, 18 Dec

Castle

🕐 Apr–Sep, Tue–Sun 10–1, 4–7; Oct–Mar, Tue–Sun 10–1, 3–5

💰 Cheap

🗺 28C2

✉ Carretera Cap Blanc–Llucmajor

☎ 180155

🕐 Fri–Wed 10–5

🍴 Near by (£)

💰 Cheap

Capdepera's castle dominates the views of the town as you approach

CASTELL D'ALARÓ (► 19, TOP TEN)

CASTELL DEL REI ✪

The hike to this remote mountain castle, 7km north of Pollença, is one of the most popular in Mallorca; it gets particularly crowded because of the limited hours. The castle is on a large private estate and it is only open to visitors on Saturday. Walk from Pollença to avoid parking problems; allow at least five hours for the round trip. You get there by taking the small country road to Ternelles opposite Pollença's Roman bridge; stay on this road until it ends at the gate to the estate. The walk then climbs gently through a cool pine forest, eventually reaching the castle, 490m above sea level. Founded by the Moors and strengthened by Jaume I, this was the last fortress to surrender to Pedro of Aragón when the brief-lived kingdom of Mallorca came to an end. It has been abandoned since 1715 and would be terribly romantic if it were not for the crowds.

➕ 29D5
🕐 Path open Mar–Dec, Sat 8:30–12; you must leave by 3
🚌 Palma–Pollença
💲 Free
↔ Pollença (► 66)

COLÒNIA DE SANT JORDI ✪

Once the port for the market town of Campos, Colònia de Sant Jordi is now a busy resort, on a rocky promontory close to Mallorca's southern tip. Its small beach looks out over several islets, with good views all the way to Cabrera (► 46). There are two further sandy beaches to the east, and the long stretch of Platja Es Trenc begins just west of town. To the north are the hot springs and spa hotel of Banys de Sant Joan. The main reason for coming here, though, is to take the boat trip to Cabrera.

➕ 29D2
🍴 Choice of restaurants
🚌 From Palma
↔ Cabrera (► 46), Ses Salines (► 85)
❓ Market held Wed

Watersports and sandy beaches at Colònia de Sant Jordi

In the Know

If you only have a short time to visit Mallorca, or would like to get a real flavour of the island, here are some ideas:

10
Ways To Be A Local

Try to learn a little of the language, Catalan as well as Spanish – a simple *bon dia* goes a long way.

Relax, take your time and settle into the Mediterranean way of life.

Take a siesta to avoid the afternoon sun – have a long lunch, or rest in the shade.

Do everything late – a late lunch, a late supper, a very late night.

Join the evening *passeig* to see and be seen – put on your best clothes and pop into a bar for *tapas* and a chilled sherry.

Change out of your beachwear for restaurants, shops and churches – Mallorcans rarely dress formally but they always manage to look smart.

Find a local *festa* and get swept along with the crowd.

Go walking in the mountains at weekends, or join a *romería* (pilgrimage) to a hilltop church.

Respect the local environment – don't drop litter or pick wild flowers.

Drink your coffee strong and sweet, with a touch of brandy, whatever the time of day.

10
Good Places To Have Lunch

Bon Lloc (£) ✉ Carrer Sant Feliu 7, Palma ☎ 718617. You won't find better value than this four-course vegetarian lunch. 🕒 Tue–Sat.

Caballito de Mar (££–£££) ✉ Passeig Sagrera 5, Palma ☎ 721074. Fish restaurant perfectly placed to catch the winter sun.

Celler Sa Font (££) ✉ Plaça d'Espanya 18, Sineu ☎ 520313. Where the farmers go after Sineu's Wed market. 🕒 Closed Thu.

Centre d'Accio Catolica (£) ✉ Avinguda Bisbe Campins 13, Porreres. Huge portions, excellent food, ridiculous prices – in a church hall.

Es Verger (££) ✉ on the way to Castell d'Alaró ☎ 510002. Farmhouse restaurant specialising in roast lamb from a wood-burning oven. 🕒 Closed Mon.

La Gran Tortuga (££) ✉ Aldea Cala Fornells 1, Peguera ☎ 686023. Eat and swim on a terrace overlooking the sea. 🕒 Closed Mon.

Santa Marta (££) ✉ Carrer Bellavista 1, Fornalutx ☎ 631952. The place to dine with a view. 🕒 Closed Tue.

S'Escar (££) ✉ Platja Es Trenc, Ses Covetes ☎ 838273. Pizza and paella beside a nudist beach.

Stay (£££) ✉ Moll Nou, Port de Pollença ☎ 864013. Fresh fish beside the harbour.

Port de Sóller, seen from the Mirador de Ses Barques

Taberna de la Boveda (££) ✉ Passeig Sagrera 3, Palma ☎ 720026. Great *tapas* on the waterfront. ⊙ Closed Sun.

10
Top Activities

Birdwatching: the best areas are the S'Albufera wetlands, the salt flats around Ses Salines, and Gorg Blau and Cúber reservoirs between Sóller and Lluc.

Cricket: have a game with the MCC – Magaluf Cricket Club (☎ 682880).

Cycling: bike hire is available in resorts and at Ciclos Bimont, Plaça Progrés 19, Palma (☎ 450505).

Fishing: you need a licence – enquire at tourist offices.

Golf: there are 11 courses (► 113).

Horse riding: several centres have classes for all abilities. Contact Federació Balear Hípica, Carrer Garita 21, Palma (☎ 404073).

Sailing: more than 40 marinas. The national sailing school is at Avinguda Joan Miró, Cala Major (☎ 402512).

Scuba diving: clubs in Palma, Port d'Andratx and Santa Ponça (► 114).

Tennis: Federació Balear de Tenis, Costa de Sa Pols 6, Palma (☎ 720956).

Walking: especially in the Serra de Tramuntana. Take a map, compass, sun hat and plenty of water.

5
Good Beaches

- Cala Millor
- Es Trenc (nudist)
- Formentor
- Magaluf
- Platja de Palma

10
Best Viewpoints

- Castell d'Alaró
- Coll de Sóller, Palma–Sóller road
- Ermita de Bonany
- Mirador de Ses Animes, Banyalbufar
- Mirador de Ses Barques, Sóller–Lluc road
- Passeig Marítim, Palma
- Puig de Randa
- Puig de Santa Eugènia
- Puig de Teix, near Deià
- Santuari de Sant Salvador

5
Quiet Coves

- Cala Deià
- Cala Fornells (Peguera)
- Cala Mesquida (north of Capdepera)
- Cala Tuent (near Sa Calobra)
- Portals Vells

53

COVES D'ARTÀ (► 21, TOP TEN)

COVES DEL DRAC (DRAGON CAVES)

CUEVAS
DEL
DRACH

➕ 29E3
☎ 820753
🕐 Apr–Oct, tours on the hour 10–5 (not 1); Nov–Mar, tours at 10:45, 12, 2, 3:30
🍴 Café (£)
🚌 From Palma and Port d'Alcúdia
♿ None
💷 Moderate
↔ Porto Cristo (► 74), Coves dels Hams (► below), Acuàrium de Mallorca (► 109)

Dank, dark and humid, these limestone caves on the edge of Porto Cristo have become one of Mallorca's top tourist sights. Groups of several hundred people at a time are herded along 2km of slippery paths by guides who tell you in four languages how to interpret the bizarre stalactite formations – a cactus here, a flag there, the Fairies' Theatre, Diana's Bath... You might just think they resemble thousands of spiky parsnips hanging from the ceiling. Try to imagine how Walt Disney would conjure up a fabulous witches' cave and you have the idea. The one-hour tour ends with a floodlit, floating violin concert on Lake Martel, Europe's largest underground lake, named after the French geologist Édouard Martel who first explored these caves in the late 19th century at the commission of Archduke Ludwig Salvator. Afterwards you can return by boat across the lake to the exit.

COVES DELS HAMS

➕ 29E3
✉ Carretera Manacor–Porto Cristo
☎ 820988
🕐 Daily 10:30–1:15, 2:15–5
🍴 Café-restaurant (£)
♿ None
💷 Expensive
↔ Porto Cristo (► 74), Coves del Drac (► above)

You cannot miss these caves as you drive from Manacor to Porto Cristo. Most people only want to visit one set of caves and the giant billboards and flags at the entrance are an attempt to ensure that this is the one. In fact you are better off continuing to the Coves del Drac (see above) or up the coast to the Coves d'Artà (► 21). But for serious speleologists, here are the facts. The caves were discovered by Pedro Caldentey in 1905 and the electric lighting was added by his son. Their name means 'fish-hooks', which the stalactites are said to resemble. You get a guided tour and, yes, another concert on an underground lake.

DEIÀ (► 22, TOP TEN)

ERMITA DE BONANY ✪✪

This hilltop hermitage is where Junípero Serra preached his last sermon in Mallorca before leaving to found the Mexican and Californian missions. The views from the terrace, covering almost the entire plain, are superb. You can stay here in simple cells, but unlike other monasteries it has no restaurant or bar – just a chapel, a shop selling religious trinkets and a drinks machine.

✚ 29D3
☎ 561101
⚑ Free
↔ Petra (▶ 64)

> ### Did you know ?
>
> Bon any *means good year.*
> *The first church was built here in 1604; five years later, during a drought, the villagers of Petra climbed to the chapel to pray for rain. When their prayers were answered with a* bon any, *they named their sanctuary Bonany.*

FELANITX ✪

Felanitx is at the centre of Mallorca's second wine-producing area and it is also known for its capers, or 'green pearls'. You can buy them at the Sunday morning market, which spills out onto the streets around the church of Sant Miquel, with local pottery displayed on the church steps. The church façade contains a memorial to 414 people who died when a wall collapsed in 1844; further up, beneath the rose window, you can see the archangel Michael standing on the Devil's head.

✚ 29E3
🍴 Bars and cafés (£)
🚌 From Palma and Porto Colom
↔ Santuari de Sant Salvador (▶ 82)
❓ Market held Sun; Sant Agusti, *cavallets* horse dances, 28 Aug

FORNALUTX ✪✪

Fornalutx, in the hills above Sóller, calls itself the prettiest village in Spain, and it is hard to disagree – unless you accept the claims of its neighbour Biniaraix. There are several terrace restaurants and bars, where you can sit and soak in the views of olive and orange groves climbing ever higher until they reach the pine-clad foothills of Puig Major.

✚ 28C4
🍴 Several restaurants (££)
↔ Sóller (▶ 86)

The prettiest village in Spain? Go and judge for yourself

🕂 72B2
✉ Carrer Joan de Saridakis 29, Cala Major
☎ 701420
🕙 15 May–15 Sep, Tue–Sat 10–7, Sun 11–3; 16 Sep–14 May, Tue–Sat 11–6, Sun 11–3
🍴 Café (£)
🚌 4 from Palma
♿ Good
💵 Moderate

FUNDACIÓ PILAR I JOAN MIRÓ ✪✪

The painter and sculptor Joan Miró spent most of his life in Barcelona, but both his wife and mother were Mallorcan and he always longed to return to the scene of his childhood holidays to draw inspiration from what he called 'the light of Mallorca'. In 1956, aged 63, he bought a house and studio in Cala Major. He lived here until he died in 1983 after which it was enlarged to hold a permanent exhibition of his works.

The collection includes more than 100 paintings, 25 sculptures and 3,000 studio pieces but only a small amount is displayed at any time. The paintings are almost childish, all vivid splashes of bright primary colours, influenced by his love of peasant traditions and his fascination with *siurells* (clay whistles). Anyone tempted to remark that their child could do better should take a look at the heavily realistic work that Miró was producing aged eight – the fantasy came later. Works on display include the draft for UNESCO's *Mural del Sol* in Paris.

Glance into Miró's studio, left untouched since his death, with work in progress, open tins of paint and black stains all over the floor.

The Wind amongst the Bulrushes *by Joan Miró (1971)*

🕂 28B3
🍴 Two bars (£)
La Reserva (➤ 76)

GALILEA ✪✪

This pretty village, 460m above sea level, in the shadow of the great peak of Puig de Galatzó, gets crowded out by day-trippers who come to sample the views from the church terrace. On a good day you can see far out to sea, while eating *tapas* outside the church and listening to the echo of sheep-bells on the hillsides. The nearby village of Puigpunyent is also justifiably popular and is surrounded by orange groves – as well as being the base for visiting La Reserva (➤ 76).

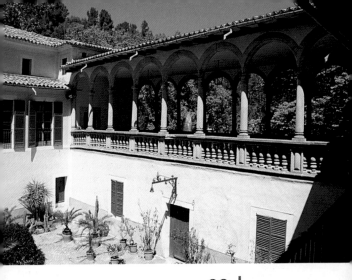

LA GRANJA ⭐⭐

This country house, just south of Banyalbufar, is on a site known since Roman times for its natural spring. When Jaume I conquered Mallorca he divided the island into four feudal estates, giving one to Count Nuno Sanç, who settled at La Granja. In 1239 the Count handed the estate to Cistercian monks to found Mallorca's first monastery. Since 1447 it has been a private house owned by various noble families; most of what you see today dates from the 17th century.

Highlights of the tour include an aristocratic drawing-room with its own theatre, the family chapel, and a dungeon with a torture chamber – but the real reason for visiting La Granja is to learn about rural Mallorcan traditions. Workshops, cellars and kitchens contain displays of everyday objects. And on Wednesday and Friday afternoons, women in traditional costume give demonstrations of lacemaking, embroidery and spinning, donkeys turn threshing-wheels and there are tastings of cheese, wine, sausages, doughnuts and fig cake. Look carefully and you just might see a tray of *coca* (Mallorcan pizza) being removed from the restaurant oven and carried to the medieval kitchens to be served beside a log fire. There are also displays of bagpipe music and folk dancing, which are entertaining if not terribly authentic.

Escape from the tour groups by walking in the grounds, which contain botanical gardens, waterfalls and a thousand-year-old yew – there is a 1,200-m signed walk. And look out for the exhibit listed in the guide as 'dog' – it is just that, a *ca de bestair*, or black-coated Mallorcan guard dog on a chain.

If you have not gorged yourself on free samples, the restaurant serves good Mallorcan staples like *pa amb oli* and *sopes mallorquines*.

✚	28B4
☎	610032
◷	Apr–Sep, daily 10–7; Oct–Mar, daily 10–6
🍴	Restaurant (£)
🚌	From Palma
♿	None
💷	Expensive
↔	Banyalbufar (▶ 46)
❓	Folk fiesta, Wed, Fri 3–5

The estate at La Granja has been turned into a living museum, where staff dressed in folk costume give displays of Mallorcan traditions

INCA ⊙

Mallorca's third-largest town styles itself 'city of leather', and if you come on an organised tour you will undoubtedly be taken to a leather factory. Shop around; the bargains these days are few and far between. Better to come on Thursdays, when the streets around Plaça d'Espanya are taken over by Mallorca's largest weekly market. Plenty of leather here, of varying quality, plus jewellery, carved olive-wood, lace and fresh produce from across the island. Plaça d'Espanya itself becomes an open-air flower show. Near here are a smart coffee-house, Café Mercantil, with uphol-stered leather chairs, and Ca'n Delante (Carrer Major 27), one of Mallorca's top pastry shops. Inca is also known for its *cellers*, old wine-cellars turned into restaurants featuring traditional dishes at reasonable prices.

JARDINS DE ALFÁBIA ⊙⊙

These classical gardens by the entrance to the Sóller tunnel are a legacy of the Arab talent for landscaping and irrigation. Their name derives from *al fabi*, 'jar of olives' in Arabic. They were probably designed by Benihabet, the Muslim governor of Inca who converted to Christianity following the Spanish invasion.

A flight of steps lined with tall palms leads to a covered walkway – from here you can strike off to see lily ponds, bamboo groves or citrus trees growing in the shadow of the mountains. If you have just driven over the Coll de Sóller and are in need of a rest, this would make a lovely spot for a siesta. Take a book or some postcards, find a seat in the shade, then drift off to sleep to the sound of gently flowing water.

LLUC (➤ 23, TOP TEN)

LLUC-ALCARI ⊙

You could easily miss Mallorca's smallest village, which consists of little more than a bend in the Deià–Sóller road. With just a handful of houses and a hotel, it would make an ideal base for a walking holiday in the nearby mountains. The views are postcard-perfect – in fact you are far more likely to see it on a postcard than you are to actually go there. Picasso once lived in the village during a short stay on Mallorca.

LLUCMAJOR ✪

This ordinary country town, the largest in southern Mallorca, has a place in history – it was the site of the battle in 1349 where Pedro IV of Aragón killed his relative Jaume III to end Mallorca's brief spell as an independent kingdom. Jaume's death is commemorated by a statue at the end of Passeig Jaume III. Near by, on Carrer Obispo Taxaquet, is another statue in honour of Llucmajor's cobblers. Shoemaking is still a significant industry here. Almonds and apricots grow around the town and make good buys at the market, held twice a week in Plaça d'Espanya.

➕ 28C3
🍴 Cafés and bars (£)
🚌 From Palma
↔ Puig de Randa (➤ 75)
❓ Market held Wed, Sun

MAGALUF ✪

More than anywhere else in Mallorca, Magaluf has been blighted by the curse of mass tourism. During the 1980s it became a byword for all that was wrong with Mallorca; foreign TV crews would flock here to film drinking competitions, wet T-shirt contests and teenagers throwing up on the beach. In the 1990s Magaluf has tried hard to change its image. High-rise hotels have been destroyed, a new seafront promenade has been built, and the council has introduced activities from guided walks to *tai chi* on the beach. But still the lager louts come... and if you want cheap sun, sea, sand and *sangría*, there's no better place.

➕ 28B3
🍴 Huge choice of bars and restaurants (£)
🚌 Regular buses from Palma
↔ Palma Nova (➤ 63), Portals Vells (➤ 72)

Magaluf – never mind the lager louts, the beach is superb

🕂 29E3

🍴 Several bars and cafés (£)

🚌 From Palma and Porto Cristo

❓ Market held Mon

Perlas Majórica

✉ Avinguda Majórica 48

☎ 550200

🕐 Mon–Fri 9–1, 2:30–7, Sat–Sun 10–1

🎟 Free

Setting pearls into their gold surrounds at a factory in Manacor

MANACOR ✪

Mallorca's second city is the nearest thing the island has to an industrial town. Despite the lack of obvious sights, the narrow streets behind the church make a pleasant place to stroll and soak up the atmosphere of everyday Mallorca. The church, Església dels Delors de Nostra Senyora, was built on the site of a mosque and its minaret-style tower can be seen for miles. Look inside to see the figure of Christ with scrawny hair and a skirt – pilgrims queue up to kiss his bloodstained feet.

Almost every visitor to Manacor ends up at a pearl factory – **Perlas Majórica** is the best-known. Mallorca's artificial pearl industry produces 50 million pearls a year, using the scales of a million fish, so do not imagine they are a safe alternative for your vegetarian friends. They are said to be indistinguishable from the real thing, and almost as expensive.

🕂 29D3

🍴 Restaurants and bars (£)

🚌 From Palma

🔄 Algaida (▶ 43), Vilafranca de Bonany (▶ 90)

❓ Market held Mon; Sant Bartomeu festival, 24 Aug; Fira de la Perdiu (partridge and hunting fair), first Sun in Dec

MONTUÏRI ✪

High on a ridge surrounded by old stone windmills, the village of Montuïri is probably the most impressive sight along the Palma–Manacor road. The eight mill-towers of the Molinar district, redundant since the 1920s, are the symbol of the village; the best views are from the Ermita de Sant Miquel, a 19th-century hermitage on top of a small hill 2km to the east. Montuïri is the setting for one of Mallorca's most spectacular festivals: each August *Cossiers*, accompanied by dancers with bagpipes, flutes and drums, dress up as women and devils and perform a dance, the origins of which stretch back at least 400 years, where evil is overcome by good.

The Northeast

This leisurely half-day drive takes in several family attractions close to the northeast coast. It can easily be done as a day-trip from Palma, adding 1½ hours to the time.

Begin by the OlivArt factory shop, as you enter Manacor on the C715 from Palma. Follow signs to Porto Cristo, leaving Manacor along a boulevard with palm trees down the middle.

After 13km you see the Coves dels Hams (► 54) – choose between stopping here or continuing to Porto Cristo for the Coves del Drac (► 54).

The road continues to Porto Cristo, where you turn left at the seafront up a steep hill, following signs to Son Servera and Cala Millor.

The road leads through orchards divided by drystone walls, reaching Auto-Safari (► 45) where you can drive around the zoo.

A word in your ear – you never know who you might meet on a drive around Auto-Safari

Continue north, bypassing Cala Millor and turning left into Son Servera. Turn right towards Capdepera (► 50).

Long before you get there you see the castle crowning the village on a hill. Stop here for lunch and a climb to the castle, then if you feel like an afternoon on the beach take the side road to Cala Mesquida.

Otherwise take the C715 to Artà.

Again you see the town long before you get there. After exploring Artà (► 45), take to the coast.

Follow the C712 coast road around the bay of Alcúdia.

You pass the S'Albufera nature reserve (► 77) before finally reaching Alcúdia (► 16).

Return to Palma in under an hour by taking the C713 and joining the motorway at Inca.

Distance
80km

Time
4 hours including visits to a cave and the zoo

Start point
Manacor
✚ 29E3

End point
Alcúdia
✚ 29D5

Lunch
Café l'Orient (£)
✉ Plaça de l'Orient, Capdepera
☎ 563098

✚ 29D4
🍴 Bars and cafés (£)
❓ Market held Sun; Revelta de Sant Antoni, 16–17 Jan

Museu Etnòlogic de Mallorca
✉ Carrer Major 15
☎ 717540
🕐 Tue–Sat 10–2, 4–7, Sun 10–2
🍴 Cheap

Visit the museum to see its collection of siurells

MURO ✪✪

This small town between Inca and the S'Albufera marshes has one overriding attraction – the **Museu Etnòlogic de Mallorca**. This museum, housed in a former mansion, gives fascinating glimpses into Mallorca's past. The kitchen contains pottery similar to what you see in the markets today; the recreated pharmacy has a pair of scales in the shape of a crucifix. Upstairs there is a fine collection of *siurells* (clay whistles) featuring men on horseback, carrying water and playing guitars. A courtyard with a well, a waterwheel and orange trees leads to more exhibits – blacksmith's and cobbler's workshops, a collection of carriages, and tools once used by silversmiths, sculptors and spoonmakers.

The Catalan-Gothic church of Sant Joan Baptista looks almost Arabic, guarded by palm trees and a tall, square bell-tower linked to the main church by a tiny bridge. Rebuilt in the 16th century, it has a colourful rose window over the west door. Another church, the convent of Santa Anna, used to stage fights between bulls and bulldogs, and bullfights can still be seen at the Plaça de Toros, built out of white stone in its own quarry in 1910.

Sa Pobla, 4km north of Muro, is Mallorca's vegetable basket; this fertile area of marshes reclaimed as farmland is referred to as 'the land of a thousand windmills'. It is also the home of one of Mallorca's most unusual festivals, the Revelta de Sant Antoni. For two days each January pets are led through the town to be blessed outside the church, dancers drive out the Devil for the coming year, and everyone eats pastries filled with spicy spinach and marsh eels.

MUSEO DE MALLORCA SECCION ETNOLOGICA

ORIENT ⊗⊗

Nervous drivers should not even think about tackling the road to Orient from Bunyola, with bends at alarming angles and little in the way of barriers to stop you tumbling to your death (there is a much easier approach from Alaró). But those who make it to this village are rewarded with a marvellous sight – one of Mallorca's tiniest hamlets, with a population of less than 30, nestling among olive trees at the foot of Puig d'Alfábia. Orient is popular with walkers – numerous walks start from here, including an ascent to Castell d'Alaró – and with weekend day-trippers from Palma, who visit its three restaurants for Sunday lunch.

PALMA NOVA ⊗

There are people who can remember when this was just a village; then along came the tourist boom, and 'new Palma' became the favoured resort of the British. More restrained than Magaluf, less exclusive than Portals Nous, Palma Nova occupies a prime position on the western side of the bay of Palma. It makes a good base for a family holiday, with nearby attractions including Marineland and Aquapark (▶ 108) – as long as you don't mind sharing your family holiday with a thousand others.

PEGUERA ⊗

This beach resort, popular with German tour operators, was the first in Mallorca to have its own artificial beach, created from imported sand. Once on the main road from Palma to Andratx, it has become much more peaceful since the construction of a bypass and the opening in 1996 of a seafront promenade. Just outside Peguera is Cala Fornells, a chic resort of terracotta houses set around a pretty cove.

➕ 28C4
🍴 Three good restaurants (££)
 Castell d'Alaró (▶ 19)

Orient is a favourite spot for mountain walkers, cyclists and lovers of Mallorcan cuisine

➕ 28B3
🍴 Wide choice of restaurants (£–££)
🚌 Regular buses from Palma
 Magaluf (▶ 59), Portals Nous (▶ 72)

➕ 28B3
🍴 Wide choice of restaurants (£–££)
🚌 From Palma

63

The house in Petra where Junípero Serra was born has been preserved much as it would have been in the 18th century

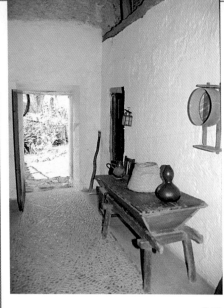

PETRA ⭐⭐

This sleepy town of sand-coloured houses would be completely off the tourist map if it were not the birthplace of Mallorca's most famous son, Fray Junípero Serra. Born in 1713, he became a priest in 1730 and worked as a missionary in Mexico from 1749 to 1763. At the age of 54 he was sent to California; the missions he established there grew into some of the USA's largest cities, including San Diego and San Francisco.

You can visit the **house** where Serra's parents lived, a **museum** devoted to his life and work, the font where he was baptised (in the church of Sant Pere) and a plaque, outside the same church, describing him as 'explorer, missionary, hero, civiliser'. Anyone walking down the street leading to his birthplace, decorated with majolica tiles depicting him baptising Native Americans, might be inclined to disagree, but by the standards of his day he was certainly a hero.

PLATJA DE PALMA ⭐

If you cannot wait to get on a beach, this 5-km stretch of fine white sand is just minutes from the airport. The two resorts of Can Pastilla and S'Arenal have merged into one, connected by a long palm-lined promenade offering every possible entertainment in summer. This is a good resort for families – there are children's playgrounds and first-aid stations, and a 'tourist train' runs the length of the promenade. Take a *passeig* here before dinner and you have a fabulous view of Palma, the twinkling lights on the waterfront reflected in the sea.

+ 29D3
🍴 Es Celler restaurant (££); bars on main square (£)
🚌 From Palma
↔ Ermita de Bonany (▶ 55)
❓ Market held Wed

Serra House and Museum
✉ Carrer Barracar Alt
☎ 561149
🕐 By arrangement – follow the directions to the keyholder's house
💷 Donation requested

+ 73C2
🍴 Wide choice of bars and restaurants (£–££)
🚌 Regular buses from Palma

The Plain

This lovely drive criss-crosses the central plain, following old Roman roads through almond and apricot groves on its way to several small market towns.

Start in Petra, following signs to Santa Margalida from the parish church. Bypass Santa Margalida by bearing left towards Muro.

In Muro (▶ 62), Carrer Major takes you to the museum – well worth a visit.

Continue along Carrer Major, over a crossroads and past the church of Sant Joan Baptista towards Sa Pobla.

Next you cross a fertile land of windmills, red earth and potato fields. Up ahead you see the mountains.

From Sa Pobla, follow signs to Llubi; when you reach Llubi go uphill into the village and down again to reach a main road. Cross the road and take the narrow track towards Sineu.

Drystone walls to either side line the route to Sineu (▶ 86). On entering the town note the modern sculpture in the street as you pass beneath it.

Follow signs to Sant Joan. As you enter Sant Joan, turn right to Montuïri (▶ 60) – worth a brief stop.

Leaving Montuïri, cross the Palma–Manacor highway by the Orquídea pearl shop and head for Porreres (▶ 67). A short detour takes you up to the Santuari de Montesió.

Leave Porreres in the direction of Vilafranca de Bonany (▶ 90). Turn left in Vilafranca and pass Els Calderers on your right.

You could visit the stately home of Els Calderers, taking a short cut to Sant Joan.

Take the next right turn to Sant Joan, from where you can return to Petra,

There are excellent views of the Ermita de Bonany and of Petra's church as you approach.

Distance
81km

Time
3 hours

Start/end point
Petra
✚ 29D3

Lunch
Centre d'Accio Catolica (£)
✉ Avinguda Bisbe Campins, Porreres

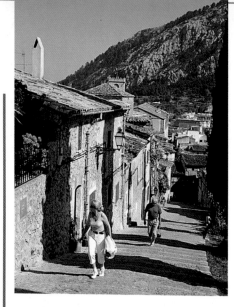

Climbing the Calvari steps on the way to salvation, with Puig de Maria in the background

🚩 29D5

🍴 Excellent cafés and restaurants (££)

🚌 From Palma

🔁 Castell del Rei (➤ 51), Port de Pollença (➤ 70), Puig de Maria (➤ 74)

❓ Market held Sun; classical music festival, Jul–Sep; *Devallement* procession, Good Fri; *Moros i Cristians*, mock battle, 2 Aug

Municipal Museum

☎ 530015

🕐 Tue, Thu, Sun 10–1

♿ Donation requested

POLLENÇA ✪✪✪

At the eastern end of the Serra de Tramuntana and tucked between two hills, each topped by a sacred site, Pollença is the perfect Mallorcan town. Large enough to avoid being twee but small enough to wander round in a morning, it has none of the feel of other towns which have succumbed under the sheer weight of tourism. Foreigners have long been attracted here, but Pollença has learned to accept and adapt to tourism without losing its soul. Café life is still the rule; if you want to join in, come on a Sunday morning when the Plaça Major is filled with market stalls and the locals congregate after church to relax in the Café Espanyol.

The Pont Romà (Roman bridge) on the edge of town gives a clue to Pollença's long history. The name Pollença dates from the 14th century, when settlers from Alcúdia named the town after their former Roman capital. Among many historic buildings is a former Jesuit convent, now the town hall. From here you climb 365 steps, lined with cypress trees, to reach the Calvari church, with its ancient wooden cross and views of Puig de Maria (➤ 74). The Calvari steps are the scene of a moving procession each Good Friday, when a figure of Christ is removed from a cross and carried down the steps by torchlight.

The **municipal museum** in the former Dominican convent contains the remains of prehistoric sculptures shaped like bulls, as well as a *mandala* (Tibetan sand painting) given by the Dalai Lama in 1990. The cloisters of the convent are the venue for Pollença's celebrated classical music festival.

PORRERES ✪

Porreres is typical of the small towns on the Mallorcan plain – nothing much to see, but an easy-going atmosphere and a good place to while away a couple of hours. The main street, Avinguda Bisbe Campins, runs from the church to the town hall and is lined with bars and cafés. Inside the town hall is a small modern **art gallery** with two works by Salvador Dalí. Just outside Porreres is a former hilltop hermitage, **Santuari de Montesió**, with a simple chapel, irregular cloisters and views across the plain and out to sea. You can stay here in very basic rooms.

+ 29D3
☎ Art gallery: 647725;
Sanctuary: 647185
🕐 Art gallery: Tue
10:30–12:30
🍴 Choice of restaurants and bars (£)
💰 Art gallery: free
❓ Market held Tue

PORT D'ALCÚDIA ✪

As the name suggests, this was once just a port serving a city – now the port has completely outgrown the town that it serves. The biggest of the resorts on Mallorca's northeast coast, it stands at the head of a 10-km stretch of sandy beach which continues around the bay of Alcúdia as far as Can Picafort. The area around the fishing harbour is the most attractive; the promenade on Passeig Marítim faces a row of fish restaurants. Near here is the commercial port, where passenger ferries leave for the Menorcan city of Ciutadella.

+ 29D5
🍴 Wide choice of restaurants (££)
🚌 From Palma and Alcúdia; also from Port de Pollença in summer
↔ Alcúdia (► 16)

PORT D'ANDRATX ✪✪

Dress up to come here, or you will feel seriously out of place. Port d'Andratx is one of Mallorca's classiest resorts, popular with the yachting fraternity and with film stars whose Italian-style villas can be seen climbing up the hillsides. But don't let that put you off; come here all the same. The harbour is one of the prettiest in Mallorca and a table at one of the waterside bars is really the perfect place to watch the sunset.

+ 28A3
🍴 Wide choice of restaurants (££–£££)
🚌 From Andratx
↔ Andratx (► 43)

Port d'Andratx, where the yachting set like to meet

Food & Drink

Mallorcan cuisine, based on pork, fish and vegetables with generous use of garlic and olive oil, is hearty peasant fare steeped in tradition and rooted in local ingredients.

Good *Tapas*
- *Datiles con bacon* – dates wrapped in bacon
- *Mejillones relleñas* – stuffed mussels
- *Pimientos de Padrón* – small chillies deep-fried with salt
- *Pulpo gallego* – Galician-style octopus with olive oil
- *Tortilla española* – cold potato omelette

Not long ago every village would celebrate the *matança*, the winter slaughter of pigs, with songs and dancing and the making of hams and sausages for the coming year. Sausages come in several varieties – *sobrasada* (raw minced pork with hot red pepper) and *botifarró* (cured pork with blood), as well as spicy *chorizo* from Spain. And no bar would be complete without its *jamón serrano*, a whole cured ham displayed on an attractive slicing-board.

Mallorcan Specialities

A side effect of the *matança* was *frit mallorquí*, a fry-up of the most perishable offal with potatoes, onions and tomatoes. Nowadays you find it on menus alongside *tumbet*, a Mallorcan-style ratatouille of aubergines, potatoes and peppers in olive oil, and *sopes mallorquines*, a thick broth of thinly-sliced brown bread and vegetables. Other classic dishes include *llom amb col* (pork wrapped in cabbage with pine nuts and raisins) and *lechona asada* (roast suckling pig).

Paella is not a Mallorcan dish but it is widely available; *paella ciega* (blind man's *paella*) comes without bones. The local equivalent is *arròs brut* ('dirty rice'), saffron rice cooked with chicken, pork and vegetables. Fish is mostly imported and frozen – restaurants have to state this – but lobster, prawns, sardines and sea bass are all good. The latter, baked in rock salt, is a Mallorcan speciality.

Desserts are not Mallorca's strong point – often the choice is between *helado* (ice-cream) and *flan* (crème caramel). An interesting alternative is *gato de almendras*, almond cake served with toasted almond ice-cream. Mallorcans are very proud of *ensaimadas*, fluffy, spiral-shaped pastries dusted with sugar and filled with anything from pumpkin jam to *sobrasada* sausage; the secret ingredient is said to be the lard in the pastry. Cheeses include Mahón from Menorca and Manchego from central Spain as well as local varieties.

Sobrasada *sausages (above) and* ensaimadas *(left) are treated with a reverence normally reserved for works of art*

Wine

The *vi* or *vino de la casa* will invariably be Mallorcan, but most bottled wine is imported from Spain. The best red wines come from La Rioja – wine labelled *crianza* is aged in oak for at least a year, *reserva* for two, *gran reserva* for three. Penedés red and white wines from Catalunya are good value; Cava, Spanish sparkling wine, is from the same area. But don't disparage Mallorcan wines – the best stand comparison with anything at the same cost from mainland Spain.

Other Alcoholic Drinks

Spanish and imported beer (*cerveza*) are available everywhere – for draught beer, ask for *una caña*. Sherry is always *fino* – dry and chilled. Spanish brandy (*coñac*) comes in a bewildering variety of bottles and is added to coffee at any time of day. Leading brands include Fundador, Magno and Soberano. Gin is manufactured on Menorca – ask for Xoriguer brand. Local liqueurs include *hierbas secos* (dry) and *hierbas dulces* (sweet), both based on aniseed and packed full of herbs.

Soft Drinks

Tap water is safe but everyone drinks mineral water – *con gas* is sparkling, *sin gas* is still. Freshly-squeezed orange juice (*zumo de naranja*) is refreshing and delicious. An unusual local drink is *orxata* or *horchata*, almond milk. *Café solo* is a small shot of strong black coffee; *café con leche* comes with hot milk and *carajillo* has brandy added. Tea (*té*) is invariably a tea-bag. If you want something less stimulating, ask for *manzanilla* (camomile) or *poliomenta* (peppermint tea).

🔲 29D5
🍴 Wide choice of restaurants (££)
🚌 From Palma, Pollença and Alcúdia; also from Port d'Alcúdia and Cap de Formentor in summer
🔄 Alcúdia (➤ 16), Cap de Formentor (➤ 18), Pollença (➤ 66)
❓ Market held Wed

PORT DE POLLENÇA ✪✪

This genteel, old-fashioned resort at the mouth of Pollença bay is particularly popular with families, and with older visitors in winter. There is also a large community of foreign residents, mostly retired British. The promenade along Passeig Voramar, all whitewashed villas and pine trees leaning into the sea, is perfect for an early evening walk. Look out for the bust of Hermen Anglada-Camarasa, the Catalan painter who spent many years in Pollença and whose work is displayed in the Fundació la Caixa in Palma (➤ 33). A favourite walk from Port de Pollença is the 3-km hike across the Formentor peninsula through the Bóquer valley, a paradise for ornithologists and lovers of wild flowers.

> ### Did you know ?
>
> Port de Pollença has long been the favoured resort of the British middle classes, who would stay at its water-front hotels enjoying casual flirtations and games of bowls on the beach. The British crime writer Agatha Christie captures this world in a 1936 short story, Problem at Pollensa Bay.

PORT DE SÓLLER ✪✪

This small resort, set around a fish-shaped natural harbour, has the only beach of any note along the entire north coast. It is the starting-point for several boat trips along the coast; the trip to Sa Calobra (➤ 78) is one of the few to run throughout the year. Port de Sóller is also a good base for walks. A climb of less than an hour brings you to Cap Gros lighthouse for panoramic views of the bay and the mountains behind; a longer path, through rock gardens and olive groves, connects with an old mule track from Deià to Sóller.

🔲 28C5
🍴 Wide choice of restaurants
🚌 From Palma, Valldemossa and Deià
🚋 From Palma; tram from Sóller
🔄 Sóller (➤ 86)

A Day Out by
Train & Tram

The opening of a railway line from Palma to Sóller in 1912, and a tram linking Sóller to its port the following year, brought the northwest coast within easy reach of the capital. The vintage carriages are still in use, providing a joyride for tourists and a relief for locals from the terrors of the Palma–Sóller road. Five trains a day leave from Plaça d'Espanya in Palma – the 10:40 is labelled the *turistico* but all you get for the extra cost is a more crowded train and a short photo stop.

The train, all mahogany panels and brass fittings, leaves Palma amid a bustle of hisses, hoots and whistles before rattling down the city streets and into the suburbs.

Soon you are out on the plain, passing small country stations and pigs rooting beneath the trees. You can get off at Bunyola and visit the Tunel factory where Mallorca's herb-based liqueurs are made – the label shows a train emerging from a tunnel.

Stay on the train and soon you start to climb, entering a 3-km tunnel before returning to daylight for the drop, through a dizzying series of bends, to Sóller (➤ 86).

Time
1½ hours each way

Start point
Plaça d'Espanya, Palma
✠ 35D4
🚌 Most city and island-wide buses terminate here

End point
Port de Sóller
✠ 28C5

Lunch
Tapas bars (£)
✉ Plaça Constitució, Sóller

The 'Orange Express' tram to Port de Sóller runs hourly, connecting with the arrival of the train. Stand on the platform as it clatters through orchards and back gardens and you can imagine you are living 50 years earlier.

It takes 20 minutes to complete the 5-km journey to the port. If you do not want to return the same way, buses leave from the jetty for Palma via Deià and Valldemossa.

Take the toytown train from Palma to Sóller (above), then hop on a tram to its port (left)

BADIA DE PALMA

Son Espanyol •
Establiments

La Reserva ■

3   Galilea •
Galatzó •   *613m*
                         ▲ *Na Baùçana*
          • Son Claret
                                        Son Anglada
                                        Son Roca • Es Se
                                                   de la H
                                        Son Vida • Sa Vileta
                                                   Son Serra
                                        Son Rapinya
                                                   Poble
                                                   Espany
  • Es Capdellà

                                        Coves de   Castell de
                    Calvià   Gènova ■   Bellver
                                                 ■   ■
                         Serra de Na Burguesa   *485m* Cala
2   Gènova •   Majo
                                        Fundació Pilar
  • Son Vic Nou   i Joan Miró ■
                    Son Pieres •   Sant Agusti
                                        Portals C719 Cas Català
                                        Nous ■ • Ses Illetes
Peguera ■
                         C719   PM1 ■ **Marineland**
                                      ■**Palma Nova**
Santa   *Platja de Palma Nova*
Ponça ■   *184m* **Magaluf**
                   ▲   **Aquapark**

  Es
  Malgrat   • Sa Porrassa

                         Cove de la
                         Maré de Déu ■
1   *164m*
                   ▲   • Portals Vells
         Cala
Illa del */Rafaubetx*
Toro   Cap de Cala Figuera

        A   **B**

✚ 72B2
🍴 Wide choice of bars and
   restaurants (££–£££)
🚌 21 from Palma
↔ Palma Nova (► 63), Ses
   Illetes (► 85)

PORTALS NOUS   ✪

This is one of the more exclusive resorts in the bay of
Palma – not many high-rise hotels here, just rows of
private villas and apartments dominating the shoreline.
Puerto Portals marina, opened in 1987, is the summer
home of the jet-set. King Juan Carlos has been known to
moor here, and the younger royals can be seen
frequenting the waterfront restaurants and bars. Don't
even think about looking in the smart boutiques unless you
have a high credit card limit. More ordinary mortals can
make do with a visit to Marineland (► 109).

✚ 28B3
🍴 Beach bar and restaurant
   (££)
🚌 From Palma on Wed &
   Fri (☎ 717190)

PORTALS VELLS   ✪✪

A bumpy track from Magaluf leads through pine woods to
this beautiful cove at the southwest tip of Palma bay. In
summer it gets crowded, but out of season you could have
your own private beach, with golden sand, rocky cliffs and
shimmering turquoise water. In fact there are two
beaches; the smaller one, El Mago, is Mallorca's official
nudist beach. From the main beach, hike along the cliffs to
the Cove de la Mare de Déu, a rock chapel built by
fishermen to give thanks for a safe landing. Back on the
road, another 2km brings you to the headland of Cap de

Cala Figuera, where you look back at sweeping views of the entire bay of Palma.

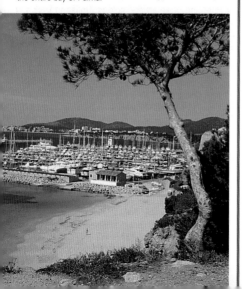

How the other half lives – the glitzy marina at Puerto Portals looks across the water to the mass-market resorts at Palma Nova and Magaluf

PORTO COLOM ★

This fishing village, once the port for Felanitx, was named in honour of Christopher Columbus, who is said – without much evidence – to have been born here. Until the late 19th century Porto Colom was busy supplying wine to France; but when phylloxera killed the vines, its role as a port diminished and it has only recently discovered a new life as a tourist resort. Popular with Mallorcan and Spanish visitors and set inside a deep natural harbour, it still has the feel of a small fishing port with boats around the quay and pastel-coloured houses lining the waterfront, each with its own landing-stage. Cala Marçal, 2km south, has a wide sandy beach leading to a narrow rocky cove.

PORTO CRISTO ★

This was one of the main resorts on the east coast until Cala Millor came along. So much the better: with bigger and better beaches elsewhere, Porto Cristo has carved out a role as a friendly, family resort, taking advantage of a superb position at the end of a long, sheltered inlet. Once the port for Manacor, Porto Cristo was the only place in Mallorca to be caught up in the Spanish Civil War, when it was briefly captured by Republican forces in 1936. There is not much to do but swim, sunbathe and dine at the terrace restaurants which are perfectly placed to catch the lunchtime sun – but day-trippers come in droves to visit the nearby caves (▶ 54). Other nearby family attractions include an aquarium and a safari park (▶ 108).

PÒRTOL ★

The neighbouring villages of Pòrtol and Sa Cabaneta, between Palma and Santa Maria del Camí, have become something of an artists' colony. Unlike in Deià and Banyalbufar, though, the artists are Mallorcan – potters taking advantage of the rich local soil. The only reason for coming here is to visit the *ollerías* (workshops), where prices are much lower than in the tourist shops. Good buys include *greixoneras* (heavy earthenware cooking pots) and *ollas* (clay storage jars), as well as simple brown-glazed plates and *plats morenos*, glazed bowls painted with symbols (some of the designs go back to Arab times). Several artists specialise in the clay whistles called *siurells*.

PUIG DE MARIA ★★

Climb for an hour out of Pollença, or drive up a terrifying potholed road, and you are rewarded with views over Cap de Formentor and the entire northeastern coast – as well as back down over Pollença. Nuns settled on Puig de Maria ('Mary's mountain') in 1371 and remained for several hundred years, refusing to leave even when the Bishop of Palma ordered them down for their own safety. The convent is still there, on top of the mountain; the chapel smells of incense and the refectory of woodsmoke. You can stay in simple cells in the sanctuary here, but don't expect luxury – you pay extra if you take a shower. The caretaker will rustle up a *paella* to save you the long walk back to town.

PUIG DE RANDA ✪✪✪

This table mountain, rising 543m out of the plain, has been a place of pilgrimage ever since Ramón Llull (➤ 14) founded Mallorca's first hermitage here in 1275. He came aged 40, shaken by an incident which caused him to review his way of life. Bent on seduction he chased a married woman through Palma on horseback; unable to shake him off, she lifted her blouse to reveal cancerous breasts. Llull retired in isolation to Puig de Randa to ponder a life of youthful excess. These days pilgrims to Puig de Randa are as likely to be weekend cyclists in search of a challenge as seekers after religious truth. The winding road to the summit leads to three separate hermitages. The lowest, Oratori de Nostra Senyora de Gràcia, is perched on a ledge in the cliff above a sheer 200-m drop. Further up is the Santuari de Sant Honorat and finally Santuari de Cura, where Llull lived. The sense of history is somewhat offset by the radio mast on the mountain-top and the electric candles in the church, but this is still a special place. Visit the Sala Gramàtica to see Llull's original manuscripts and a bottle of 1934 Chartreuse made in the monastery, then look out from the terrace at the views of the plain, with Palma Bay and the isle of Cabrera in the distance. Simple rooms are available in a modern pilgrims' block.

➕ 29D3
☎ 660994
🍴 Restaurant at Santuari de Cura (££)
🖐 Free

Randa, the village at the foot of the mountain. The climb from here to the summit is one of Mallorca's most testing cycle rides

75

29F3
🍴 Snack bar (£)
🚌 From Palma to Cala Millor
🎟 Free
🔄 Cala Millor (➤ 48)

PUNTA DE N'AMER ✪

This 200-hectare nature reserve on a headland jutting out from the east coast is an oasis of peace amid a desert of high-rise apartments and hotels. Once, the whole coast was like this – thankfully, environmentalists have saved this small section from development. Walk south from Cala Millor, or north from Sa Coma, on a well-defined 1.5-km track. Eventually you reach the Castell de n'Amer, a 17th-century watchtower. Have a drink at the summit and look down at what you have left behind.

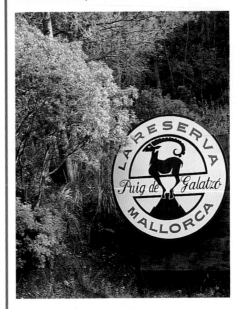

How to go walking in the mountains without getting lost – follow the easy waymarked trail around La Reserva

🔲 28B3
☎ 616622
🕐 Apr–Sep, Wed–Sun 10–8; Oct–Mar, Wed–Sun 10–6
🍴 Café (£)
🎟 Expensive
🔄 Galilea (➤ 56)

LA RESERVA

On the slopes of Puig de Galatzó near the village of Puigpunyent, this nature reserve describes itself as 'Mallorca's paradise'. A 3-km trail of waymarked paths leads you through Mallorca's mountain scenery in less than two hours, past waterfalls and springs, olive trees and charcoal stoves. A series of boards provides background information on wildlife and mountain industries. Well laid out and interesting, the reserve gives you a feeling for the area. It will seem a bit sterile if you have been out in the mountains on your own – but it might help you to make sense of what you have already seen.

S'ALBUFERA ✪✪

Just off the coast road 5km south of Port d'Alcúdia, the S'Albufera wetlands make a welcome relief from long stretches of crowded beach. Birdwatchers come from all over Europe to see rare migrants like Montagu's harriers and Eleanora's falcons; species breeding here include stonechats, moustached warblers and the long-eared owl. Ospreys leave their breeding sites on the cliffs to come here to fish; peregrines and hoopoes live here all year round.

The name derives from the Arabic for 'lagoon', but the site has been exploited since Roman times – Pliny writes of night herons, probably from S'Albufera, being sent to Rome as a gastronomic delicacy. The wetlands were drained for agriculture in the 19th century by a British company which subsequently went bankrupt; the network of canals dates from this time. Rice was introduced in the early 20th century, paper was manufactured from the reeds and sedge, and it is only since 1985, following fears that tourist development was damaging the area's fragile ecology, that S'Albufera has been a protected nature reserve. There are footpaths, cycle trails, birdwatching hides and an audio-visual display room where you can listen to birdsong.

➕ 29D4
✉ Carretera Port d'Alcúdia–Artà, km5
☎ 892250
🕐 Apr–Sep, daily 9–7; Oct–Mar, daily 9–5
🍴 Picnic area
🚌 From Port d'Alcúdia to Cala Rajada in summer
♿ Free
❓ Cars are not allowed in the reserve at weekends and are discouraged at all times – leave them 1km from the visitor centre on the main road

Get away from it all with a day at S'Albufera, walking among the marshes and listening to the birds

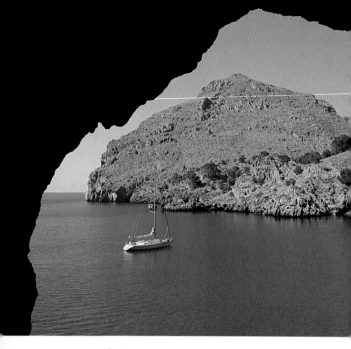

🕇 28C5
🍴 Several restaurants (£–££)
🚢 From Port de Sóller (all year, ☎ 633109)
❓ Choral concert on the beach in Jul

View through a rock arch at Sa Calobra – Mallorca's most beautiful spot, or a place spoiled by tourists?

SA CALOBRA ✪✪

Do not believe anyone who tells you that they have discovered the perfect unspoilt cove on the north coast – at least, not if its name is Sa Calobra. This is indeed a beautiful spot, which is why tour buses pour in by the dozen every day, even in winter.

The journey to Sa Calobra is as memorable as the bay itself. A twisting road around Puig Major plunges 800m in just 12km, turning 270 degrees at one point to loop under itself (a feature known as the 'Knotted Tie'). The easier approach is by boat from Port de Sóller, passing genuinely isolated bays with an excellent view of Puig Major, albeit spoilt by the military installations on the summit of Mallorca's highest mountain.

Once there, walk through 200m of tunnels to reach the Torrent de Pareis ('twin streams'), which begins several kilometres up in the mountains at the confluence of the torrents of Lluc and Gorg Blau. Up to 400m high and only 30m wide, with some sections never seeing daylight, this dramatic gorge culminates in a small pebble beach where you can picnic among the crowds. In summer, when the gorge is dry, you can hike inland between the cliffs; do not attempt this in winter.

A side turn off the road to Sa Calobra leads to Cala Tuent, a small cove with a sandy beach and a 13th-century church, Ermita de Sant Llorenç. Cala Tuent is likely to be quieter than Sa Calobra; but don't believe anyone who tells you they have discovered the *real* unspoilt cove...

SA DRAGONERA ⭐

This uninhabited island off Mallorca's western tip was the focus for a turning-point in Mallorcan history in 1977, when it was occupied by environmentalists protesting against a planned tourist development. The campaigners won, the island became a nature reserve instead, the seabirds survived, and for the first time the authorities realised that mass tourism had reached its limit.

Six kilometres long and crowned by an ancient watchtower, Sa Dragonera takes its name from its shape, said to resemble a dragon. You can visit in summer by boat from Sant Elm; in winter you have to make do with views of the dragon from the beach at Sant Elm or from the climb to Sa Trapa (► below).

➕ 28A3
🚢 From Sant Elm Mar–Sep
(☎ 246698)
↔ Sant Elm (► below)

From Sant Elm you can climb to an abandoned monastery or take a boat to Sa Dragonera

SANT ELM ⭐⭐

The main reason for visiting Sant Elm, a laid-back resort with a fine sandy beach, is for the views of Sa Dragonera (► above). You can take a boat to the island from the jetty at the end of the main street, or sit outside the fish restaurants on the same jetty.

A popular walk from Sant Elm leads to the abandoned Trappist monastery of Sa Trapa. Set out on Avinguda de la Trapa and climb through coastal *maquis* and pine, with fine views of Sa Dragonera. The round trip takes about three hours; a shorter route is signposted beside the cemetery on the Sant Elm to Andratx road. Near here is the village of S'Arracó, built by Spanish settlers returning from the American colonies, with houses in colonial *Indianos* style.

➕ 28A3
🍴 Choice of restaurants
(££)
🚌 From Andratx or Peguera
🚢 From Port d'Andratx and
Peguera
↔ Sa Dragonera (► above)

SANTA EUGÈNIA

28C4
Local bars (£)
One or two buses daily from Palma
Market held Fri

People argue over whether the mountains or the coast represent 'the real Mallorca', but the heart of the island is to be found in villages like this. The bars are frequented by local farmers and make few concessions to tourism; there is nothing to see as such, just marvellous views across to the *serra* where the mountains rise out of the plain and you can just make out the white sanctuary church above the ruins of Castell d'Alaró (▶ 19) in the distance. The old 6-km cart track to Sencelles offers good walking and more views, over the postcard village of Biniali.

SANTA MARIA DEL CAMÍ

28C4
Bars and cafés (£)
From Palma and Inca
Market held Sun

This market town on the Palma–Inca railway has developed a reputation as one of Mallorca's artistic centres. Most of the island's potters work close by, in Pòrtol (▶ 74), and Santa Maria is the centre of manufacture of *roba de llengues* ('cloth of tongues'), cotton woven into bright zigzag patterns and used in curtains, bedspreads and upholstery. Just off the main square is Ca'n Conrado, former Carmelite cloisters and a peaceful retreat from the traffic on the Palma road.

SANTA PONÇA ·

28B3
Bars and restaurants (£–££)
From Palma
Rei en Jaume regatta in Jul

Santa Ponça may look like just another beach resort but it has a permanent place in Mallorcan history. It was here that Jaume I landed in 1229 to begin his conquest of Mallorca, a conquest he described as 'the best thing man has done for a hundred years past'. A relief on a large cross above the marina, erected in 1929, records the event.

A Walk from Santa Eugènia

This simple walk gives spectacular views for the minimum of effort.

Leave the village of Santa Eugènia and head in the direction of the market town Santa Maria del Camí. After 1km turn left along a narrow lane to Ses Coves.

The lane bends left, then descends, and you see Ses Coves ('the caves'), used at various times as pirate hideaways and wine cellars. One of them still contains an ancient wine-press.

When the road divides, fork left; soon you reach some iron gates at the entrance to a track on your right.

After going through these gates you enter Puig d'en Marron, and climb until the road runs out.

Continue along a mud track, keeping right at each fork, until you emerge onto a wide open plateau. Return to the iron gates by the same route and turn right along the lane. Follow this lane briefly uphill then take the second track on the left.

After passing an arched entrance to a well, turn immediately left through an orchard towards a house.

To the right of the house, the wall is marked with a red dot; climb from here to a pass.

Here you can clamber over a stone wall to your left to reach the cross on the summit of Puig de Santa Eugènia. This is the high point of the walk, with wonderful views that stretch across the plain to the mountains in the distance. On the opposite clifftop is one of Mallorca's oddest sights – the cockpit of a broken-up plane.

Retrace your steps to the stone wall and then follow the path that leads through the bushes on your left. When you reach a tarmac road, turn right. The first left returns you to Santa Eugènia.

Distance
7km

Time
2 hours

Start/end point
Santa Eugènia
 28C4
From Palma – only one or two buses per day, so check timetable

Lunch
Ca Na Cantona (£)
Carrer Balenguera, Santa Eugènia

SANTANYÍ ⭐

Do not be surprised if the buildings in Santanyí look just that little bit more mellow than everywhere else – this small town is the source of the golden sandstone used in Palma's cathedral and La Llotja among others. The old gate, Sa Porta Murada, seen as you enter the town from Palma, is a good example of Santanyí stone and a reminder that this was once a walled town. The parish church of Sant Andreu Apòstel contains a massive rococo organ, designed by Jordi Bosch and brought here from a convent in Palma. The streets around the church are the focus for one of Mallorca's liveliest markets.

SANTUARI DE SANT SALVADOR ⭐⭐

This old hermitage, 509m above sea level at the highest point of the Serra de Llevant, was the senior house of Mallorca's monastic order and the last to lose its monks, in 1992. It is still a popular place of pilgrimage, flanked by two enormous landmarks – to one side a 14-m stone cross, to the other a 35-m column topped by a statue of Christ holding out his right hand in blessing. The church contains a fine carved alabaster retable, but more interesting is the side chapel off the gatehouse, full of poignant mementos

The views from the Santuari de Sant Salvador stretch right across the central plain

and prayers to Our Lady. Like other former monasteries, Sant Salvador has a few simple rooms available for pilgrims.

The views from the terrace take in Cabrera, Cap de Formentor and several other hilltop sanctuaries dotted across the plain. From the statue of Christ you look out towards the Castell de Santueri, a 14th-century rock castle built into the cliffs on the site of a ruined Arab fortress.

SERRA DE TRAMUNTANA ✪✪✪

The 'mountains of the north wind' which run the length of Mallorca's north coast are home to the island's most spectacular landscapes. Pine-covered slopes almost lean into the sea; as you climb higher, forested hills give way to barren crags and peaks. The people of Mallorca have good reason to be grateful to the mountains. In winter they act as a buffer, shielding the plain from the fierce *tramuntana* wind and absorbing most of the island's rain and snow; in summer they provide a cool retreat from the heat of Palma and the south.

The Serra de Tramuntana runs for 88km from Andratx to Pollença, with the rocky outcrops of Sa Dragonera and Cap de Formentor at either end. Of ten peaks over

✚ 28C4

↔ Lluc (▶ 23), Fornalutx (▶ 55), Sa Calobra (▶ 78), Sóller (▶ 86)

❓ Walking, birds, spring flowers

Fresh air, walking and sea views – the Serra de Tramuntana mountains (above) and Cap de Ses Salines (right)

1,000m, most are concentrated in the area around Lluc; the highest are Puig Major (1,445m) and Puig Massanella (1,349m). There are no rivers, though there are several mountain torrents which swell rapidly after rain – and the Cúber and Gorg Blau reservoirs, essential resources on an island so often affected by drought.

The mountains are best seen slowly, on foot; you smell the wild rosemary, hear the sheep-bells, frighten the goats, breathe in the air and marvel at pine trees growing out of red rock, a divine version of the colours of Mallorcan village houses. If you have to drive, take care – the roads here are the most dangerous on the island, and the endless procession of hairpin bends requires total concentration. The most dramatic drive of all is the C710 from Sóller to Lluc, traversing tunnels and gorges on its way between Puig Major and Puig Massanella.

SES COVETES ✪

The name of this village means 'small caves' and this is believed to refer to Roman burial chambers on the same site. Nowadays people come here for one thing – to get to Platja Es Trenc, a 3-km stretch of fine white sand backed by gentle dunes. This has long been an unofficial nudist beach, even during the puritanical Franco era. It no longer has the hippy atmosphere of old, but it still makes a peaceful, less commercial contrast to some of the other beaches on the south coast.

29D2
S'Escar beach bar/restaurant (££)
From Palma, Jun–Sep, daily 9:30

SES ILLETES ⭐

This genteel resort, with its white villas and old-fashioned hotels, is for many people the most attractive in the whole Badia de Palma. Two small beaches look out over a pair of *illetes* (islets), the larger one crowned by an old watchtower. Its proximity to Palma means that you will never be alone here; in summer the buses from Palma to Ses Illetes are packed out at weekends. But if you want a base near the capital, combining a city break with a beach holiday, this could be just the place.

➕ 72B2
🍴 Cafés and restaurants (££)
🚌 3 from Palma
↔ Cala Major (▶ 47), Portals Nous (▶ 72)

SES PAÏSSES ⭐

Although not as extensive as the ruins at Capocorb Vell (▶ 50), this Bronze Age settlement near Artà is still a significant site and a link with Mallorcans of 3,000 years ago. Most impressive of all is the massive entrance portal, formed from three stone slabs weighing up to eight tonnes each. Inside there are several rooms and an *atalaia* (watchtower); the entire settlement is surrounded by a Cyclopean drystone wall.

➕ 29E4
🕐 Apr–Oct, Mon–Fri 9–1, 4–7, Sat 9–1; Nov–Mar, Mon–Fri 9–1, 2:30–5, Sat 9–1
🚌 From Cala Rajada or Palma then a short walk
💷 Cheap
↔ Artà (▶ 45)

SES SALINES ⭐

This small town between Santanyí and Colònia de Sant Jordi is named after the nearby saltpans, which act as a magnet for migrant waders and wildfowl on their way from Africa to their breeding grounds in Europe each spring. Cap de Ses Salines, Mallorca's southernmost point, is another good spot for birdwatching. The town itself makes a pleasant place to stroll, with an abundance of local Santanyí sandstone which turns golden in the sun. Just outside Ses Salines, on the road to Santanyí, is **Botanicactus**, one of Europe's largest botanical gardens, with bamboo and palm trees and, extraordinarily diverse in form, dozens of varieties of cactus.

➕ 29D2
🍴 Bars and cafés (£)
🚌 Between Colònia de Sant Jordi and Santanyí
↔ Colònia de Sant Jordi (▶ 51), Santanyí (▶ 82)
🛒 Market held Thu

Botanicactus
✉ Carretera Ses Salines–Santanyí
☎ 649494
🕐 Apr–Sep, daily 9–7; Oct–Mar, daily 9–6
💷 Moderate

85

29D4
🍴 Several restaurants (££)
❓ Market held Wed

S'Estació
✉️ Carrer Estació
☎️ 520750
🕐 Mon-Fri 9:30–1, 4:30–7:30; Sat 9:30–1
🎟️ Free

The winged lion, honouring St Mark, is the symbol of Sineu

SINEU ✪✪✪

Sineu, at the geographical centre of Mallorca, comes alive each Wednesday morning at the island's most traditional market. It takes place on several levels. The sound of bleating leads you to the livestock market, where weather-beaten farmers haggle over the price of sheep before heading for the town's *celler* restaurants for an early brunch. Further up, on the way to the church, you pass the symbol of Sineu, a winged lion; near here are numerous stalls selling leather, lace and pearls. Eventually you reach Sa Plaça, the church square, where the action is liveliest of all, as local housewives turn out to buy the week's food. Buckets of olives, strings of tomatoes, bags of squirming snails – they are all here, along with plenty of fresh fruit, vegetables and flowers. Get to Sineu early, before the tour buses arrive, to catch the flavour of a traditional country market. Good buys include dried figs and apricots, pottery from Pòrtol and baskets from Sudan. Also in Sineu is S'Estació, an unusual modern art gallery based in the old station.

28C4
🍴 Wide choice of bars and restaurants (£–££)
🚌 From Palma; tram to Port de Sóller
🔄 Fornalutx (▶ 55), Port de Sóller (▶ 70)
❓ Market held Sat; Moros i Cristians, re-enactment of a 1561 battle in which local women helped to defeat a band of Turkish pirates, 8–10 May

SÓLLER ✪✪✪

Set in a lush valley of orange groves between the mountains and the sea, Sóller is popular with day-trippers who arrive on the vintage train from Palma (▶ 71) and seem to do little but sit outside the cafés in Plaça Constitució soaking up the atmosphere and the sun. With several *tapas* bars, a fine selection of pastry-shops, local ice-cream and freshly-squeezed orange juice, there is little temptation to move on.

Sóller grew rich on oranges and the results can be seen in its extravagant *modernista* architecture. The church of Sant Bartomeu has a 1912 arched tower suspended above the rose window, with spires like huge needles pointing into the air. The same architect, Gaudí's pupil Joan Rubió, designed the Banco Central Hispano next door.

A stroll to the cemetery above the station, flanked by cypress trees and filled with potted plants, gives a clue to Sóller's history. Several of the epitaphs are in French, revealing the significant French community of the town, descendants of those who came to make their fortune by exporting oranges.

Sóller has two museums worth visiting. The **Natural Science Museum**, in a turn-of-the-century manor house on the Palma road, has a collection of fossils and a botanical garden. The **Museu Municipal** is an 18th-century manor house in the town centre, filled with antiques and relics of old Sóller.

A final word of advice: come here by train, rather than car. The climb over the Coll de Sóller, with its 57 hairpin bends, is the most terrifying drive in Mallorca. There is now a controversial new road tunnel through the mountain if you must drive, but the train journey is a delight so why not give yourself a treat.

Sóller's main square (above) contains some interesting modern architecture, such as the bank designed by Joan Rubió (left)

Natural Science Museum
- ✉ Carretera Palma–Port de Sóller
- ☎ 634064
- ⏰ Apr–Sep, Tue–Sat 10:30–1:30, 5–8, Sun 10:30–1.30; Oct–Mar, Tue–Sat 10–2, 3:30–5, Sun 10:30–1:30
- 💲 Cheap

Museu Municipal
- ✉ Carrer Mar 9
- ☎ 630200
- ⏰ Mon–Fri 11–1, 5–8
- 💲 Cheap

📍 28B4

✉ Carretera Valldemossa–
Deià

☎ 639158

🕐 Mon–Sat 9:30–2,
3–sunset

🍴 Mirador de Na Foradada
(££)

🚌 From Palma, Valldemossa
and Port de Sóller

👝 Cheap

🔗 Deià (► 22)

❓ Sunset concerts in
summer

SON MARROIG ⬤⬤

Of all the famous foreigners attracted to Mallorca's northwest coast, none is so admired locally as 'S'Arxiduc', Archduke Ludwig Salvator. Born in 1847 in the Pitti Palace, Florence, the son of Leopold III of Tuscany and Marie Antoinette de Bourbon, he came to Mallorca 20 years later to escape from Viennese court life and immediately fell in love with the island. An ecologist before it was fashionable, and an early hippy who wore Mallorcan peasant clothes, he bought up estates along the coast in an effort to save them from development, and devoted himself to studying and recording Mallorcan wildlife and traditions. His seven-volume *Las Baleares* took 20 years to produce and is still an authority on its subject. He died in 1915 in a Bohemian castle.

The Archduke's home at Son Marroig, outside Deià, has been turned into a shrine to his memory, with his photographs, paintings and books and a museum devoted to his life. In the gardens is a white marble rotunda, made from Carrara marble and imported from Italy, where you can sit and gaze at the Na Foradada ('pierced rock') peninsula, jutting out to sea with a gaping 18-m hole at its centre. Ask at the house for permission to walk onto the peninsula.

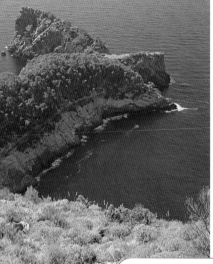

Private view – the Archduke's garden looks down over the peninsula of Na Foradada

Did you know ?

When the Archduke fell in love with a local carpenter's daughter, he bought her the neighbouring estate of Miramar, along the coast on the way to Valldemossa.
Another of his estates, S'Estaca, now belongs to the actor Michael Douglas.

VALLDEMOSSA (► 26, TOP TEN)

The Archduke's Bridlepath

This walk was mapped out by Archduke Ludwig Salvator during tours of his estates by mule; as well as spectacular coastal views, it gives an introduction to traditional mountain industries. You pass *sitjas* (round charcoal ovens), *casas de neu* (snow pits where winter snows were stored beneath a layer of ash), *forns de calç* (lime kilns) and *caças a coll* (thrush nets slung between the trees).

Begin by walking through the car park opposite Bar Sa Mata on the main road through Valldemossa. Turn right into Carrer Joan Fuster, then first left and onto a rough track at the top of the hill.

You climb gently at first, towards a group of pines, then more steeply, following red waymarks to a clearing. From here it is a short, tough climb to a mirador and the start of the Camí de S'Arxiduc, marked by a ruined stone refuge.

Follow the waymarks onto a high plateau and continue for about two hours.

For the best views of all, a one-hour diversion (just as the main path bears round to the right to begin its descent) takes you to the summit of the Teix, from where most of Mallorca is visible on a clear day.

The path drops back down to Valldemossa through a wooded valley, passing a shelter where you can camp in summer.

This walk is for experienced walkers only. Take food and water, a map, compass and whistle, and protection from sun, wind and rain. The weather on the mountains can change very quickly.

For a shorter walk to the foot of the Teix, you can simply do the final section in reverse. Leave Valldemossa by walking past Son Gual, the large old house with a tower, and turn left after 10 minutes onto a wide track, signposted 'refugi'. The climb through the valley to the shelter and back will take a couple of hours if you walk briskly.

Distance
13km

Time
6 hours

Start/end point
Valldemossa

✚ 28B4
🚌 From Palma, Deià or Port de Sóller

Lunch
Take a picnic

29D3
From Palma and Manacor
Market held Wed

Els Calderers
Carretera Palma–
Manacor, km37
526069
Apr–Sep, daily 10–6;
Oct–Mar, daily 10–5
Café (£)
Moderate

Vilafranca is famed for its melons and sun-dried tomatoes

VILAFRANCA DE BONANY

As you drive through this small town on the road from Palma to Manacor, you cannot help noticing the strings of vegetables hanging outside several of the shops – peppers, aubergines, garlic and, above all, tomatoes. These are the famous *tomàtigues de ramallet*, sold on their stalks to be spread over *pa amb oli*. Vilafranca is also known for its honeydew melons, whose harvest is celebrated with a large melon festival each September. The other reason for coming here, apart from food, is to visit **Els Calderers**, a manor house between Vilafranca and Sant Joan. This was once at the centre of a great wine estate but like so many others it fell victim to the phylloxera disease. Reopened in 1993, the 18th-century house is now a museum of Mallorcan furniture and traditions; you can visit the wine cellar, granary, bakery, chapel and wash-house as well as wander around the main house with its paintings, guns and toys.

Where To...

Palma

Prices
Prices are approximate, based on a three-course meal for one without drinks and service:

£ = under 2,000 pesetas
££ = 2,000–4,000 pesetas
£££ = over 4,000 pesetas

Most restaurants serve a *menú del día* at lunchtime (► 96) which will usually work out much cheaper. It is normal practice to add about 10 per cent to the bill as a tip.

A Warning
Opening hours change frequently, and many restaurants take an annual holiday in winter. It is always a good idea to telephone before setting out.

Asador Tierra Asanda (££)
Barbecued meat – suckling pig, lamb, kid – in an old Palma mansion close to Avinguda Jaume III.
✉ **Carrer Concepció 4**
☎ **714256** ⏱ **Lunch, dinner. Closed Wed, Sun dinner**

Baisakhi (££)
High-class Indian cuisine; try the gourmet menu, with wine and *lassi* included.
✉ **Passeig Marítim 8**
☎ **736806** ⏱ **Lunch, dinner. Closed Sun**

La Bodeguilla (££)
Classic Castilian stews amid hanging wine bottles; the same owners have a stylish *tapas* bar next door.
✉ **Carrer Sant Jaume 2**
☎ **718274** ⏱ **Lunch, dinner. Closed Sun**

Bon Lloc (£)
Vegetarian restaurant with good-value four-course set lunch.
✉ **Carrer Sant Feliu 7**
☎ **718617** ⏱ **Lunch Tue–Sat, dinner Fri 9–11**

La Bóveda (££)
Good range of *tapas* and the best *pa amb oli* in Palma.
✉ **Carrer Boteria 3**
☎ **714863** ⏱ **Lunch, dinner. Closed Sun**

Caballito de Mar (££)
Popular fish restaurant on the seafront – sit outside to catch the winter sun.
✉ **Passeig Sagrera 5**
☎ **721074** ⏱ **Lunch, dinner daily**

Ca'n Carlos (££)
One of the few restaurants in central Palma to focus on traditional Mallorcan cuisine.
✉ **Carrer de l'Aigua 5**
☎ **713869** ⏱ **Lunch, dinner. Closed Sun**

Ca'n Eduardo (££)
Traditional fish restaurant above the fish market.
✉ **Es Moll de Pescadors**
☎ **721182** ⏱ **Lunch, dinner. Closed Sun, Mon**

Ca'n Joan de S'Aigo (£)
Classy café where Joan Miró used to go for hot chocolate, ice-cream and *ensaimadas*.
✉ **Carrer Sant Sanç 10**
☎ **710759** ⏱ **Closed Tue**

Casa Gallega (££)
Galician *tapas* and all-you-can-eat seafood buffet.
✉ **Carrer Pueyo 2 and Passeig Marítim 25** ☎ **714377; 284974**
⏱ **Lunch, dinner daily**

Celler Sa Premsa (£)
Mallorcan classics in a converted garage lined with wine vats and faded bullfighting posters.
✉ **Plaça Bisbe Berenguer de Palou 8** ☎ **723529** ⏱ **Lunch, dinner. Closed Sun**

Es Parlament (££)
Elegant restaurant in the ground floor of the Balearic Parliament building – a favourite haunt of politicians, famed for its black *paella*.
✉ **Carrer Conquistador 11**
☎ **726026** ⏱ **Lunch, dinner. Closed Sun**

Fundació la Caixa (££)
Cocktails, cakes, sandwiches and serious meals in the bar of the former Gran Hotel.
✉ **Plaça Weyler 3** ☎ **728077**
⏱ **Lunch, dinner. Closed Sun dinner**

Giovanni's (££)
This busy Italian restaurant near La Llotja has become a

Palma institution, popular both with tourists and foreign residents.

✉ **Carrer Sant Joan 3**
☎ **722879** 🕐 **Lunch, dinner. Closed Mon**

Koldo Royo (£££)
Basque *nouvelle cuisine* with a Michelin star.
✉ **Passeig Marítim 3**
☎ **457021** 🕐 **Lunch Mon–Sat, dinner Mon–Fri**

La Lubina (££)
Fish restaurant on the quay – try *lubina en sal*, sea bass baked in rock salt.
✉ **Es Moll Vell** ☎ **723350**
🕐 **Lunch, dinner daily**

McDonalds (£)
For those who must find a McDonalds wherever they go, the one in Palma is at the top of the Born.
✉ **Plaça Rei Joan Carles I 7**
☎ **718485** 🕐 **All day**

Mediterráneo 1930 (£££)
Expensive international cuisine – try the pigs' trotters stuffed with brains.
✉ **Passeig Marítim 33**
☎ **458877** 🕐 **Lunch, dinner daily**

Na Bauçana (£)
Friendly vegetarian restaurant with set-price midweek lunch.
✉ **Carrer Santa Bàrbara 4**
☎ **721886** 🕐 **Lunch Mon–Fri**

El Pilon (££)
Good *tapas* bar in an alley off the Born.
✉ **Carrer Ca'n Cifre**
☎ **717590** 🕐 **Lunch, dinner. Closed Sun**

Porto Pi (£££)
Haunt of the Spanish royals in an old manor house on the outskirts of Palma.
✉ **Avinguda Joan Miró 174**
☎ **400087** 🕐 **Lunch, dinner. Closed Sun**

Reixons (££)
Modern Mallorcan cuisine and classical music in a converted mansion near La Llotja.
✉ **Carrer Montenegro 1**
☎ **726327** 🕐 **Lunch Mon–Sat, dinner Thu–Sat**

S'Arrosseria (££)
Rice served in a dozen different styles, from 'convent rice' (vegetarian) to lobster *paella*.
✉ **Passeig Marítim 13**
☎ **737447** 🕐 **Lunch, dinner daily**

S'Olivera (££)
Mediterranean cooking and a large range of tapas in the heart of the old Arab quarter.
✉ **Carrer Morey 5** ☎ **712935**
🕐 **Lunch, dinner daily**

Sa Taverna (£)
The speciality here is *pa amb oli* – bread with olive oil and tomatoes, and a huge choice of toppings.
✉ **Carrer Pou 12** ☎ **454826**
🕐 **Lunch, dinner daily**

Sa Volta (£)
Authentic cellar bar with hams hanging from the ceiling – the best of numerous *tapas* bars along the same street.
✉ **Carrer dels Apuntadors 5**
🕐 **Lunch, dinner daily**

Svarta Pannan (£)
Family-run Swedish restaurant with the emphasis on old-style home cooking.
✉ **Carrer Brondo 5** ☎ **721039**
🕐 **Lunch, dinner. Closed Sun**

Tapas
Tapas are a Spanish institution. Originally a free 'lid' (*tapa*) of ham across a drink, nowadays they consist of small portions of everything from octopus to olives. Locals eat *tapas* before going out to eat, but several portions can make an unusual meal in itself. The best place to eat *tapas* in Mallorca is in the area around La Llotja in Palma.

Around the Island

Eating Out in Mallorca

The Spanish like to eat late – many restaurants do not even open until 1:30 at lunchtime and 8:30 in the evening, and fill up an hour or two later. It is a good idea to book a table in advance, especially in summer and at weekends. Formal dress is rarely necessary – even at the best establishments smart casual is the rule. And children are always welcome!

Algaida

Cal Dimoni (££)

Meat and blood sausages grilled over an open fire at the 'house of the devil'.

✉ Carretera Palma–Manacor, km21 ☎ 665035 ⬧ Lunch, dinner. Closed Wed

Ca'n Mateu (££)

Roast suckling pig and other specialities beside a pool and children's play area.

✉ Carretera Palma–Manacor, km21 ☎ 665036 ⬧ Lunch, dinner. Closed Tue

Es 4 Vents (££)

Mallorcan and Spanish classics, very popular for Sunday lunch.

✉ Carretera Palma–Manacor, km21 ☎ 665173 ⬧ Lunch, dinner. Closed Thu

Hostal d'Algaida (££)

Mallorcan cuisine in an old coaching inn – try croquettes of spinach with monkfish.

✉ Carretera Palma–Manacor, km21 ☎ 665109 ⬧ Lunch, dinner. Closed Wed

Artà

Café Parisien (£)

Coffee, pastries, *tapas* and daily specials in an arty café on the city's main street.

✉ Carrer Ciutat ☎ 835440 ⬧ Lunch, dinner. Closed Sun

Binissalem

El Suizo (££)

Swiss fondues plus French and Mallorcan cuisine.

✉ Carrer Pou Bo 20 ☎ 870076 ⬧ Lunch Wed–Mon, dinner Wed–Sun

Cala Major

Krishna (££)

Simple Indian food – for when you just can't take any more *paella*.

✉ Avinguda Joan Miró 332 ☎ 405769 ⬧ Dinner only. Closed Sun, Mon

Mariners (££)

Nouvelle cuisine at sensible prices. Popular with expats.

✉ Avinguda Joan Miró 352 ☎ 702161 ⬧ Dinner only. Closed Sun, Mon

Cala d'Or

Barraca (££)

Imaginative Spanish dishes like roast lamb with honey, served on a pretty terrace in summer.

✉ Avinguda Bélgica 4 ☎ 657978 ⬧ Dinner only, daily

El Bistro Blau y Blanc (££)

An eclectic mix – pasta, salad, chicken curry, and fondues on winter evenings.

✉ Passeig d'es Port 43, Porto Petro ☎ 658002 ⬧ Lunch, dinner daily

Port Petit (££)

Seafood specialities and unusual desserts in a smart restaurant overlooking the marina.

✉ Avinguda Cala Llonga ☎ 643039 ⬧ Lunch, dinner. Closed Mon

Cala Rajada

Ses Rotges (£££)

Quality French cooking with prices to match at one of Mallorca's top hotels.

✉ Carrer Rafael Blanes 21 ☎ 563108 ⬧ Lunch, dinner daily. Closed Nov–Apr

Calvià

Ca Na Cuco (££)

Fresh, good-value Mallorcan cuisine. Popular with locals.

✉ Avinguda de Palma 14 ☎ 670083 ⬧ Lunch, dinner. Closed Mon, Wed

Meson Ca'n Torrat (££)

Mallorcan classics like *llom amb col* and roast shoulder of lamb in a rustic bar opposite the church.

✉ **Carrer Església 5**
☎ **670682** 🕐 **Lunch, dinner. Closed Tue**

Capdepera

Café de l'Orient (£)

Lively *tapas* bar on the market square – each dish is available in three different-sized portions to make up a filling and varied meal.

✉ **Plaça de l'Orient 4**
☎ **563098** 🕐 **Lunch, dinner daily**

Castell d'Alaró

Es Verger (££)

Roast lamb cooked in a wood-fired oven at this farmhouse restaurant halfway up to the castle.

✉ **On the way to Castell d'Alaró** ☎ **510002** 🕐 **Lunch, dinner. Closed Mon**

Deià

Ca'n Quet (£££)

Basque and Mallorcan seafood specialities are served in the restaurant of Es Moli hotel.

✉ **Carretera Valldemossa–Deià** ☎ **639196** 🕐 **Lunch, dinner. Closed Mon**

El Olivo (£££)

Fine *nouvelle cuisine* in a romantic setting – probably the best restaurant on the island for a special occasion.

✉ **La Residencia hotel**
☎ **639011** 🕐 **Lunch, dinner daily**

Mirador de Na Foradada (££)

Dine with a view of the northwest coast. Typical Mallorcan/Spanish cuisine.

✉ **Son Marroig, Carretera Valldemossa–Deià** ☎ **639026** 🕐 **Lunch, dinner. Closed Thu**

Sa Dorado (££)

Fresh fish daily at this small restaurant on Deià's main street.

✉ **Carrer Arxiduc Lluis Salvador 24** ☎ **639318** 🕐 **Lunch, dinner. Closed Mon**

Sa Vinya (££)

Simple terrace restaurant offering spectacular views over the village.

✉ **Carrer Vinya Vella 3** ☎ **639212** 🕐 **Lunch, dinner daily**

Felanitx

Vista Hermosa (£££)

Galician *nouvelle cuisine* in a manor house with a pool.

✉ **Carretera Felanitx–Porto Colom, km6** ☎ **824960** 🕐 **Lunch, dinner daily**

Fornalutx

Santa Marta (££)

Fresh Mallorcan cooking and inspiring valley views.

✉ **Carrer Bellavista 1** ☎ **631952** 🕐 **Lunch, dinner. Closed Tue**

Inca

Celler Ca'n Amer (££)

This busy *celler* beside the covered market was chosen to represent Balearic cooking at the Expo 92 fair in Seville.

✉ **Carrer Miquel Duran 35** ☎ **501261** 🕐 **Lunch, dinner. Closed Sat lunch, Sun**

Celler Ca'n Ripoli (££)

Founded in 1782 with dark wooden beams, chandeliers, wine vats around the walls. Mallorcan cuisine.

✉ **Carrer Jaume Armengol 4** ☎ **500024** 🕐 **Lunch, dinner. Closed Sun**

Cellers

A *celler* is an old wine-cellar converted into a restaurant specialising in traditional Mallorcan cuisine. Real basement *cellers* have wine vats to prove it, but nowadays the term is used for any old-style restaurant. *Cellers* are good places to go in order to try Mallorcan classics like *llom amb col* (pork wrapped in cabbage) or *frit mallorquí* (fried offal). The best *cellers* are found in market towns like Inca and Sineu.

Menú del Día

Most restaurants offer a *menú del día* at lunchtime – a set-price three-course meal with water or wine included. You won't get much choice (typically soup or salad, meat or fish and fruit or ice-cream) but the food will be freshly cooked, filling and sometimes surprisingly good. A three-course lunch in a small rural town will often cost less than a single portion of *tapas* in Palma.

Jardines d'Alfábia
Ses Porxeres (££)

Catalan game dishes in a rustic barn beside the Alfábia gardens.

✉ Carretera Palma–Sóller, km9.5
☎ 613110 ⏰ Lunch, dinner. Closed Sun dinner, Mon

Orient
L'Hermitage (£££)

Choose between a flower-filled terrace or a dining-room full of antiques at this 17th-century manor house and hotel. The menu, based on fresh local ingredients, changes daily.

✉ Carretera Alaró–Bunyola
☎ 613300 ⏰ Lunch, dinner daily

Hostal de Muntanya (££)

The menu here features good-value Mallorcan classics – *pa amb oli*, roast kid, roast apples.

✉ Carrer Bordoy 6 ☎ 613380
⏰ Lunch, dinner. Closed Mon

Mandela (££)

Innovative French–Indian cuisine by a couple from Geneva, in a house at the very top of the village.

✉ Carrer Nou 1 ☎ 615285 ⏰ Lunch, dinner. Closed Sun dinner, Mon

Restaurant Orient (££)

Suckling pig is a speciality in this popular village bar.

✉ Carrer Bordoy ☎ 510248
⏰ Lunch, dinner. Closed Tue

Palma Nova
Ciro's (££)

Pizzas and other Italian/Mediterranean specialities are served on a terrace overlooking the beach.

✉ Passeig del Mar 3
☎ 681052 ⏰ Lunch, dinner daily

Gran Dragon (££)

One of the best Chinese restaurants in Spain, and the only one to be awarded three Michelin forks.

✉ Passeig del Mar 2
☎ 681338 ⏰ Lunch, dinner. Closed Sun

Peguera
La Gran Tortuga (££)

Seafood and European cuisine is served on a terrace overlooking a pretty bay – you can order your meal then take a dip in the swimming pool while it is being cooked.

✉ Aldea Cala Fornells 1
☎ 686023 ⏰ Lunch, dinner. Closed Mon

La Gritta (££)

Chic Italian restaurant with an emphasis on seafood.

✉ Aldea Cala Fornells 2
☎ 686022 ⏰ Lunch, dinner daily

Petra
Es Celler (££)

Typical Mallorcan *celler* bar with an olive press and hearty peasant cooking.

✉ Carrer de l'Hospital 46
☎ 561056 ⏰ Lunch, dinner. Closed Mon

Platja de Palma
Ca'n Torrat (££)

A treat for serious carnivores – hunks of meat are barbecued over a fire in the garden.

✉ S'Arenal exit from motorway ☎ 262055
⏰ Lunch, dinner daily

Rancho Picadero (££)

Restaurant which specialises in meats cooked on wood fires.

✉ Carrer de Flamenc 1
☎ 261002 ⏰ Lunch, dinner. Closed Mon

Pollença

Ca'n Pacienci (£££)
Sample the adventurous French-style cooking on offer here including duck in five different sauces.

✉ Carretera Pollença
☎ 532805 🕒 Dinner only, daily

Cantonet (££)
French and Spanish cooking, featuring a good range of salads and vegetarian dishes, and a bar selling snacks and sandwiches next door.

✉ Carrer Montesió 20
☎ 530039 🕒 Lunch, dinner. Closed Tue, Wed lunch

Christine en Daus (£££)
Top-quality French cooking on the Calvary steps. Several choices for vegetarians.

✉ Calvari 10 ☎ 532867
🕒 Lunch, dinner. Closed Mon

Clivia (££)
This popular restaurant is in an old manor house – the speciality is roasted sea bass.

✉ Avinguda Pollentia
☎ 533635 🕒 Lunch, dinner. Closed Tue, Wed lunch

La Font del Gall (££)
French cooking with an oriental influence.

✉ Carrer Montesió 4
☎ 530396 🕒 Lunch, dinner. Closed Mon

Port d'Alcúdia

Khum Phanit's (£)
This is a real surprise – authentic Thai cooking and extremely good value.

✉ Avinguda de la Platja 7
☎ 548141 🕒 Lunch, dinner. Closed Mon lunch

Port d'Andratx

El Patio (£££)
Nouvelle cuisine in a shady courtyard, with a five-course set menu featuring soup and sorbet.

✉ Carretera Andratx–Port d'Andratx ☎ 672013
🕒 Dinner only. Closed Wed

Miramar (£££)
Lobster and seafood beside the harbour – take out a mortgage before you come here.

✉ Avinguda Mateo Bosch 48
☎ 671617 🕒 Lunch, dinner. Closed Mon

Rocamar (££)
This is the place to try Galician and Mallorcan seafood specialities in a perfect setting at the end of the promenade.

✉ Carrer d'Almirante Riera Alemany ☎ 671261
🕒 Lunch, dinner. Closed Mon

Villa Italia (£££)
Located in an *art nouveau* hotel is this restaurant which specialises in modern Italian cuisine – how about hot strawberries with green pepper?

✉ Camino San Carlos 13
☎ 674011 🕒 Lunch, dinner daily

Port de Pollença

La Llonja del Pescado (££)
Lobster stew is a speciality at this restaurant by the harbour.

✉ Dique Moll ☎ 530023
🕒 Lunch, dinner. Closed Wed, Sun dinner

Stay (£££)
This is a popular fish restaurant on the jetty – try the *parrillada*, a fish and seafood mixed grill.

✉ Moll Nou ☎ 864013
🕒 Lunch, dinner. Dinner only Fri, Sat in winter

Fish and Seafood
Mallorca's fish stocks have long been in decline and most of the fish on sale in Mallorca is imported from mainland Spain and beyond. By law, restaurant menus should state whether fish is fresh or frozen – prices for frozen fish are invariably cheaper. Fresh fish is always excellent; specialities include lobster casserole, sea bass in rock salt, and *greixonera de peix*, a hearty fish stew cooked in an earthenware bowl.

Olives

Olives were introduced to Mallorca by the Romans and have been used ever since – the oil for cooking and soap, the branches for firewood, the wood for carving into bowls and spoons. Almost every meal begins with bread and olives, for which you may pay a small charge. Bread and olives are also at the heart of *pa amb oli*, the favourite Mallorcan snack – bread rubbed with tomato, drizzled with olive oil and topped with ham or cheese.

Port de Sóller

Celler d'es Port (££)

Enormous helpings of Mallorcan classics like roast shoulder of lamb with oregano.

✉ Carrer Antoni Montis 17
☎ 632357 ⏲ Lunch daily, dinner Sat

Sa Llotja des Peix (££)

Up-market seafood restaurant overlooking the harbour.

✉ Passeig de la Marina
☎ 632954 ⏲ Lunch, dinner. Closed Tue

Portals Nous

El Bistro de Tristan (££)

More modest version of Tristan (► below), run by the same chef and open at lunchtimes.

✉ Puerto Portals marina
☎ 676141 ⏲ Lunch, dinner. Closed Mon

Flanagans (££)

Trendy harbourside bar specialising in *paellas* and serious sandwiches.

✉ Puerto Portals marina
☎ 676117 ⏲ Lunch, dinner daily

French Coffee Shop (£)

Snacks, sandwiches and children's meals, perfectly situated next to Marineland.

✉ Carretera Palma–Andratx, km10 ☎ 676707 ⏲ Lunch, tea. Closed Tue

Meson Son Caliu (£)

Typically Mallorcan with a good-value *menú del día*.

✉ Carretera Palma–Andratx, km12 ☎ 680086 ⏲ Lunch, dinner. Closed Sun

Tristan (£££)

Nouvelle cuisine with a price tag attached – widely considered the best restaurant on Mallorca.

✉ Puerto Portals marina
☎ 675547 ⏲ Dinner only. Closed Mon

Wellies (££)

Waterside haunt of the jet set, where designer shorts are the norm. Steaks, fish, international food.

✉ Puerto Portals marina
☎ 676444 ⏲ Lunch, dinner daily

Porto Colom

Celler Sa Sinia (££)

Seafood specialities in a perfect spot on the waterfront.

✉ Carrer des Pescadors
☎ 824323 ⏲ Lunch, dinner. Closed Mon

Porto Cristo

Siroco (££)

Unpretentious fish restaurant on a terrace by the harbour.

✉ Carrer Veri 2 ☎ 820935
⏲ Lunch, dinner daily

Puigpunyent

The English Rose (££)

Small English-run restaurant beside the church – imaginative home cooking and traditional Sunday lunch.

✉ Carrer Galilea 8 ☎ 614180
⏲ Dinner Tue–Sat, lunch Sun

Son Net (££)

Spanish meets American at this country house in the mountains. Swimming pool, children's activities, guided walks before Saturday lunch.

✉ Carretera Palma–Puigpunyent, km14 ☎ 614057
⏲ Lunch, dinner. Closed Mon, Tue

Randa

Celler Bar Randa (£)

Good-value Mallorcan cuisine

in the village bar beside the church.

✉ **Carrer Església 20**
☎ **660989** ⏰ **Lunch, dinner. Closed Wed**

Es Reco de Randa (££)

Mallorcan and Spanish cooking in an old hotel at the foot of Puig de Randa.

✉ **Carrer Fuente 13**
☎ **660997** ⏰ **Lunch, dinner daily**

S'Arracó
La Tulipe (££)

Modern European cooking in a New Age arty atmosphere.

✉ **Plaça de Toledo 2**
☎ **671449** ⏰ **Dinner Tue–Sat, lunch Sun**

Santa Maria del Camí
Ca'n Moragues (£££)

High-class *nouvelle cuisine* in Read's Hotel, in a restored country house on the road to Alaró.

✉ **Carretera Santa Maria–Alaró** ☎ **140261** ⏰ **Lunch, dinner daily**

Sant Elm
El Pescador (££)

Fish restaurant on the jetty with its own fishing boat and fine views of Sa Dragonera.

✉ **Es Moll** ☎ **109198**
⏰ **Lunch, dinner. Closed Sun**

Ses Covetes
S'Escar (££)

Beach bar at the entrance to Platja Es Trenc, specialising in *paella*.

✉ **West end of Platja Es Trenc**
☎ **838273** ⏰ **Lunch, dinner daily**

Sineu
Celler Sa Font (££)

Traditional *celler* with wine vats lining the walls – very busy on market day (Wed).

✉ **Plaça d'Espanya 18**
☎ **520313** ⏰ **Lunch, dinner. Closed Thu**

Sa Boveda (££)

German, Spanish and Mallorcan cuisine in this small restaurant in a hotel cellar.

✉ **Carrer dels Bous 129**
☎ **520211** ⏰ **Dinner Wed–Mon, lunch Wed**

Sóller
Bens d'Avall (£££)

Worth it just for the sensational setting, overlooking the northwest coast. The food's not bad either.

✉ **Carretera Deià–Sóller, Urbanización Costa de Deià**
☎ **632381** ⏰ **Lunch, dinner. Closed Sun dinner & Mon, & Nov–Mar**

Ca N'Ai (££)

Traditional Spanish cooking, with fresh fish dishes in a manor house and hotel surrounded by orange groves.

✉ **Camí Son Sales 50**
☎ **632494** ⏰ **Lunch, dinner. Closed Mon**

Sa Cova (££)

Mallorcan classics (stuffed aubergines and rabbit with garlic) in a great position on Sóller's main square.

✉ **Plaça Constitució 7**
☎ **632222** ⏰ **Lunch, dinner. Closed Mon**

Valldemossa
Ca'n Costa (££)

Mallorcan and Spanish cuisine in a converted oil-mill.

✉ **Carretera Valldemossa–Deià, km2.5** ☎ **612263**
⏰ **Lunch, dinner. Closed Tue**

Coffee and Liqueurs

In Spain, *un café* after the meal means only one thing: *café solo*, served short, strong and black, with sugar. Ask for a *carajillo* and it will have brandy added, or a bottle of *coñac* left on the table for you to help yourself. If the waiter brings a liqueur with your coffee, this is a *copa*, a treat on the house. Enjoy!

99

Palma

Prices
Prices are for a double room, excluding breakfast and VAT:

£ = under 10,000 pesetas
££ = 10,000–20,000 pesetas
£££ = over 20,000 pesetas

These prices will be much lower if you book as part of a package holiday. Most hotels in the main resorts are block-booked by tour operators and it is through them that you will get the cheapest deals.

What Does It Mean?
All accommodation in Spain is strictly classified and graded by the government. Hotels are graded from one to five stars; *hostals*, with fewer facilities but often just as comfortable, from one star to three. A *hotel residencia* or *hostal residencia* is one that does not serve evening meals.

Arabella Golf Hotel (£££)
The most expensive hotel on the island, with all the luxuries you might expect. Five kilometres north of the city beside a golf course.
✉ Carrer de la Vinagrella, Son Vida ☎ 799999 🕐 All year

Born (££)
Two-star *hotel residencia* in a converted mansion near the Born. The best value if you want character in the old city.
✉ Carrer Sant Jaume 3 ☎ 712942 🕐 All year

Costa Azul (££)
If you want to stay on the waterfront, this high-rise block offers better value than most.
✉ Passeig Marítim 7 ☎ 731940 🕐 All year

Meliá Victoria (£££)
A huge modern hotel which dominates the harbour area and which has entrances onto Plaça Gomila and Passeig Marítim.
✉ Avinguda Joan Miró 21 ☎ 732542 🕐 All year

Mirador (££)
Old-fashioned waterfront hotel. Most rooms have views of the cathedral and the bay.
✉ Passeig Marítim 10 ☎ 732046 🕐 All year

Palacio Ca Sa Galesa (£££)
The embodiment of taste and luxury – a beautifully restored 17th-century merchant's house between the cathedral and the Arab baths. Rooftop terrace, help-yourself to sherry and the only indoor pool in the old city.
✉ Carrer de Miramar 8 ☎ 715400 🕐 All year

Palladium (££)
Good-value alternative a short walk from the city centre. Popular with Spanish businessmen.
✉ Passeig de Mallorca 40 ☎ 713945 🕐 All year

Pons (£)
Simple one-star *hostal residencia* in an old Palma house, with rooms arranged around a central courtyard.
✉ Carrer Vi 8 ☎ 722658 🕐 All year

Ritzi (£)
Budget *hostal* centrally located for Palma's *tapas* and nightlife quarter.
✉ Carrer Apuntadors 6 ☎ 714610 🕐 All year

San Lorenzo (££)
Six rooms only in a restored 17th-century manor house. Attractive garden with swimming pool close to the old city.
✉ Carrer Sant Llorenç 14 ☎ 728200 🕐 All year

Saratoga (££)
Modern hotel, centrally located, with a rooftop swimming pool.
✉ Passeig Mallorca 6 ☎ 727240 🕐 All year

Son Vida (£££)
Exclusive hotel in a 13th-century castle with its own golf course, 5km north of Palma.
✉ Urbanización Son Vida ☎ 790000 🕐 All year

Valparaiso Palace (£££)
You will have spectacular views over the Bay of Palma from this five-star hotel in Bonanova.
✉ Carrer Francisco Vidal ☎ 400411 🕐 All year

Around the Island

Banyalbufar

Baronía (£)
Two-star *hostal* in a former mansion with courtyard, watchtower, swimming pool and sea views.
⊠ **Carrer General Goded 16**
☎ 618146 ⏰ Apr–Oct

Mar i Vent (£)
Wonderful views from the terrace of this family-run hotel. Swimming pool and tennis court.
⊠ **Carrer Major 49** ☎ 618000
⏰ Feb–Dec

Binissalem

Scott's (£££)
Discreet British-run hotel, all antique furniture and Persian rugs, in a 19th-century town house on the church square.
⊠ **Plaça Església 12**
☎ 870100 ⏰ All year

Cala Figuera

Villa Serena (£)
Simple two-star hotel, perfectly situated at the mouth of a pretty bay.
⊠ **Carrer Virgen del Carmen 37**
☎ 645303 ⏰ Apr–Oct

Cala d'Or

Cala d'Or (££)
Ibizan-style hotel set among the pine trees overlooking the beach.
⊠ **Avinguda Bélgica 33**
☎ 657249 ⏰ Apr–Oct

Cala Rajada

Ses Rotges (££)
Old-style villa with a flower-filled garden and a Michelin-starred restaurant.
⊠ **Carrer Rafael Blanes 21**
☎ 563108 ⏰ Apr–Oct

Cala Sant Vicenç

Cala Sant Vicenç (£££)
This family-run seaside hotel near Pollença moved into the luxury bracket after a major renovation in 1996. Facilities include a sauna, gym and a heated outdoor pool.
⊠ **Cala Sant Vicenç**
☎ 530250 ⏰ All year

Castell d'Alaró

Santuari del Refugi (£)
Simple rooms in a former sanctuary on the mountain top. There are no showers or hot water but you will have wonderful views.
⊠ **Reached on foot above Castell d'Alaró** ☎ 510480
⏰ All year

Colònia de Sant Jordi

Banys de Sant Joan (£)
Thermal spa hotel opened in 1845. You can come here to treat your rheumatism or arthritis.
⊠ **Carretera Campos del Port**
☎ 655016 ⏰ Jun–Oct

Deià

Es Moli (£££)
Old-fashioned luxury hotel in a picturesque setting.
⊠ **Carretera Valldemossa–Deià** ☎ 639000 ⏰ Apr–Oct

La Residencia (£££)
A pair of 16th-century *fincas* with terraced orchards converted into a luxury hotel which is considered by many to be the best on the island. Four-poster beds and teddy bears in every suite.
⊠ **Finca Son Canals**
☎ 639011 ⏰ All year

S'Hotel d'Es Puig (££)
Featured in a short story by Robert Graves and also in Gordon West's *Jogging Round Majorca*, the 'hotel on the hill' reopened in 1996.
⊠ **Carrer Es Puig 4** ☎ 639409
⏰ All year

Reis de Mallorca

Reis de Mallorca (Kings of Mallorca) is an independent group of 18 Mallorcan hotels. It includes some of the best hotels on the island, like La Residencia in Deià, Palacio Ca Sa Galesa in Palma and the Bon Sol in Ses Illetes, but also cheaper options like the Costa d'Or in Lluc-Alcari and the Mar i Vent in Banyalbufar. What they all have in common is individuality, architectural beauty and generally excellent cuisine. Reis de Mallorca hotels can be booked on ☎ 430674.

Monasteries
Several of Mallorca's former monasteries rent out old monks' and pilgrims' cells to travellers. You may not get a shower but you will find peace, a sense of history and unforgettable hilltop views. The best known, at Lluc, is now virtually a hotel; for real solitude head instead for the Ermita de Bonany (► 55), Puig de Maria (► 74) or the Santuari de Montesió at Porreres (► 67).

Formentor
Hotel Formentor (£££)
This was Mallorca's first luxury hotel outside Palma when it opened in 1929, and it continues to set the standard for others to follow. This is a grand hotel in a beautiful setting between the beach and the pine woods, with acres of terraced gardens.
📧 **Platja de Formentor**
☎ **865300** 🕐 **All year**

Inca
Monnaber Nou (£££)
This 13th-century manor house, set in oak and pine woods to the northeast of Inca, has a name which means 'flowery fields' in Arabic.
📧 **Predio Monnaber Nou, Campanet** ☎ **877176** 🕐 **All year**

Lluc
Monestir de Lluc (£)
Comfortable accommodation in a former monastery – a popular base for walking in the Serra de Tramuntana. During the day it is packed out with tourists but by staying the night you experience a completely different side. The old pilgrim quarters and stables have been converted into apartments for long-term rent.
📧 **Lluc monastery** ☎ **517025**
🕐 **All year**

Lluc-Alcari
Costa d'Or (£)
Simple but perfect, in a magical setting above the sea. You can walk to the shore through the hotel's own pine forest.
📧 **Lluc-Alcari** ☎ **639025**
🕐 **May–Oct**

Orient
L'Hermitage (££)
Former convent turned into a select country-house hotel, with swimming pool, tennis courts, sauna and a first-class restaurant.
📧 **Carretera Alaró–Bunyola**
☎ **613300** 🕐 **Feb–Nov**

Hostal Muntanya (£)
Popular walkers' hostel in the village centre, with a restaurant serving Mallorcan classics like roast kid.
📧 **Carrer Bordoy 6** ☎ **613380**
🕐 **All year**

Port d'Andratx
Villa Italia (£££)
Over-the-top Italianate villa with marble, stucco and 'Roman pool'.
📧 **Camino San Carlos 13**
☎ **674011** 🕐 **All year**

Port de Pollença
Illa d'Or (££)
An old-fashioned hotel located at the end of the promenade.
📧 **Carrer Colón 265**
☎ **865100** 🕐 **Feb–Nov**

Miramar (£)
Small, old-style, family-run hotel on the seafront close to the town centre.
📧 **Passeig Anglada Camarasa 39** ☎ **531400**
🕐 **Apr–Oct**

Sis Pins (££)
Typically Spanish, with white walls and green shutters, this restaurant on the promenade has its own private beach.
📧 **Passeig Anglada Camarasa 77** ☎ **531050** 🕐 **Feb–Dec**

Port de Sóller
Es Port (£)
Three-star family-run *hostal*

in a 15th-century mansion with a private chapel in the courtyard. The bar has the biggest olive press you'll ever see.

✉ Carrer Antoni Montis
☎ 631650 ⏰ All year

Portals Nous
Punta Negra (£££)
Luxury hotel on a spit overlooking the marina at Puerto Portals.

✉ Carretera Palma–Andratx, km12 ☎ 680762 ⏰ All year

Puig de Randa
Es Reco de Randa (££)
Three-star hotel and well-known restaurant at the foot of the winding road to the summit.

✉ Carrer Fuente 13
☎ 660997 ⏰ All year

Santuari de Cura (£)
Rooms in the old monastery, with spectacular views from the terrace at dusk. The bar-restaurant serves simple meals.

✉ Summit of Puig de Randa
☎ 660994 ⏰ All year

Santa Maria del Camí
Read's (£££)
British-run hotel and sophisticated restaurant in a magnificent restored *finca* on the road to Alaró.

✉ Carretera Santa Maria–Alaró ☎ 140262 ⏰ All year

Santuari de Sant Salvador
Santuari de Sant Salvador (£)
Choose between the old and the modern wings of this former monastery with guinea-fowl in the yard and magnificent views over the plain. Evening meals are

available in the bar.

✉ Puig de Sant Salvador
☎ 827282 ⏰ All year

Ses Illetes
Bon Sol (£££)
Delightful family-run hotel, arranged like a wedding-cake on several levels and cascading down a hill to its own private beach.

✉ Passeig Illetes 30
☎ 402111 ⏰ Feb–Dec

Sineu
Leon de Sineu (££)
Three-star hotel in a converted town house close to the main square.

✉ Carrer dels Bous 129
☎ 520211 ⏰ All year

Sóller
Ca N'Ai (£££)
Four-star *hotel rural* in a manor house surrounded by orange groves.

✉ Camí Son Sales 50
☎ 632494 ⏰ Feb–Oct

El Guía (£)
Old-style hotel and restaurant beside the station. Excellent value.

✉ Carrer Castanyer 2
☎ 630227 ⏰ Apr–Oct

Valldemossa
Ca'n Mario (£)
Charming family-run *hostal* filled with antiques. There is a good restaurant on the first floor.

✉ Carrer Uetam 8 ☎ 612122
⏰ All year

Vistamar (£££)
Luxuriously restored *finca* with rock gardens looking down on the tiny Port de Valldemossa.

✉ Carretera Valldemossa–Andratx, km2.5 ☎ 612300
⏰ Feb–Oct

Fincas
Many of Mallorca's fincas (country estates) have recently been converted into upmarket tourist accommodation, combining character (antiques and log fires) with modern amenities like swimming pools. Some, like Ca N'Ai at Sóller, have become hotels; others, like Sa Torre, on an old wine estate near Santa Eugènia, have been turned into apartments for rent. You can get information on fincas from the Associació Agroturisme Balear, Carrer Foners 8, Palma (☎ 770336).

Markets

Weekly Markets

Almost every town in Mallorca has a weekly market; most start early and wind up by lunchtime. The larger markets all follow a similar pattern – fresh produce around the main square, specialist food stalls fanning out from there, then cheap clothes, household goods and craft stalls for the tourists. The biggest market is on Thursdays at Inca; the most traditional is the Wednesday agricultural and livestock market at Sineu.

Palma

Llotja del Peix (Fish Market)

Get here early as the night's catch goes on sale and mullet, prawns, sardines and sea bass are hawked by women with operatic voices.

⊠ **Es Moll de Pescadors**
☎ **721182** 🕓 **Mon–Sat 6AM**

Mercat Artesanal

Lively craft market on the Plaça Major, with buskers and open-air cafés.

⊠ **Plaça Major** 🕓 **Mon–Sat 10–2 in summer; Fri, Sat only in winter**

Mercat Olivar

Palma's main market, in a hall near Plaça d'Espanya. Fresh produce on the ground floor, meat and cheese upstairs, plus cheap *tapas* stalls and a public library.

⊠ **Plaça Olivar** ☎ **724650**
🕓 **Mon–Sat 7–2**

Pere Garau

Local farmers bring their produce - including live animals - to this lively market in the east of the city.

⊠ **Plaça Pere Garau**
☎ **273283**
🕓 **Mon–Sat 7–2**

Rambla

It may not match its Barcelona namesake, but Palma's Rambla is similarly lined with flower stalls.

⊠ **Passieg de la Rambla**
🕓 **Mon–Fri 8–2, 5–8, Sat 8–2**

Rastro (Flea Market)

A Palma institution which takes over part of the main ring road each Saturday morning. Plenty of bargains but lots of junk too.

⊠ **Avinguda Gabriel Alomar i Villalonga** 🕓 **Sat 8–2**

Santa Catalina

Fresh fruit and vegetable market just west of the city centre.

⊠ **Plaça Navegació**
☎ **230710**
🕓 **Mon–Sat 7-2**

Weekly Markets Outside Palma

Alaró – Fri

Alcúdia – Tue, Sun

Algaida – Fri

Andratx – Wed

Artà – Tue

Binissalem – Fri

Cala Rajada – Sat

Calvià – Mon

Campos – Thu, Sat

Capdepera – Wed

Colònia de Sant Jordi – Wed

Felanitx – Sun

Inca – Thu

Llucmajor – Wed, Sun

Manacor – Mon

Montuïri – Mon

Muro – Sun

Petra – Wed

Pollença – Sun

Porreres – Tue

Port de Pollença – Wed

Porto Cristo – Sun

Pòrtol – Wed

Santa Eugènia – Fri

Santa Maria del Camí – Sun

Santanyí – Wed, Sat

S'Arenal – Thu

Ses Salines – Thu

Sineu – Wed

Sóller – Sat

Valldemossa – Sun

Vilafranca de Bonany – Wed

Shopping in Palma

Shopping Districts

The main shopping areas in Palma are Avinguda Jaume III and the Passeig des Born for up-market boutiques (leather, antiques, designer clothes) and the pedestrian streets around Plaça Major for small specialist shops. There is also a modern shopping mall and hypermarket complex, the Centro Comercial Porto Pi, 2km from the centre.

Books

Ereso

Good selection of books about Mallorca in English and German, and a useful set of walking maps and guides.
✉ Carrer Paraires 1
☎ 726751

Fiol

Palma's leading second-hand bookshop includes a selection of foreign-language books.
✉ Carrer Oms 45 ☎ 721428

Fundació la Caixa

Art books and posters in the ground floor of this modern art gallery.
✉ Plaça Weyler 3 ☎ 728071
🕐 Mon–Sat 10–9, Sun 10–2

Ripoll

Antiquarian books and prints.
✉ Carrer Sant Miquel 12
☎ 717436

Department Stores

El Corte Inglés

Mallorcan branches of Spain's leading department store. The Club del Gourmet has an excellent range of Spanish wines, hams and cheeses.
✉ Avinguda Jaume III 15;
Avinguda Alexandre Rosselló
☎ 771760 Mon–Sat 10–10

Fancy Dress

Eurocarnavales

The place to go if you want a costume for a *festa*.
✉ Carrer Porta de Jesús 16
☎ 722627

Food

Colmado Santo Domingo

Fight your way past hundreds of hanging *sobrasada* sausages to find cheeses, fig cake and olive oil.
✉ Carrer Sant Domingo 1
☎ 714887

Forn d'es Teatre

Art nouveau shopfront and the place to buy *ensaimadas*.
✉ Plaça Weyler 11
☎ 715254

Forn Fondo

Bakery which has turned out *ensaimadas* since 1911.
✉ Carrer Unió 15 ☎ 711634

Frasquet

Go in here just to smell the melted chocolate.
✉ Carrer Brossa 19
☎ 721354

La Montaña

Sausages, hams, cheeses and one of Palma's best window displays.
✉ Carrer Jaume II 29
☎ 712595

Football

La Botiga del Barca

Mallorcans share the Spanish passion for football and Barcelona, the top Catalan side, is their nearest big-name team. This shop sells everything from Barca T-shirts and toys to cigarettes.
✉ Plaça Weyler 6 ☎ 711911

Shopping Tips

Most shops are open from around 10 to 1:30 and 5 to 8 Monday to Friday, and on Saturday mornings. The exceptions are souvenir shops in the large resorts, which stay open every day, and the Gigante chain of supermarkets, open throughout the day Monday to Saturday. Larger shops accept credit cards and travellers' cheques, but it is always advisable to have some cash.

Arts & Crafts

Siurells
Siurells are clay whistles, which have been made on Mallorca since Arab times. They come in all shapes and sizes – the most common design is a man on horseback – and are painted white with flashes of red and green. They are cheap, children love them, and the artist Joan Miró was much influenced by their brightness and simplicity.

Craft Fairs
A *Fira del Fang* (Ceramics Fair) is held each March in the town of Marratxí and all of Mallorca's leading potters are represented. Prices here are much better than in the tourist shops. *Baleart* is a Christmas craft fair held in Palma each December, with stalls selling everything 'made by hand' – from pottery and hand-made shoes to Mallorcan wines and *sobrasada* sausages.

Palma

Alpargatería Llinas
The best place to buy espadrilles (rope-soled shoes).
✉ **Carrer Sant Miquel 43**
☎ 717696

Artesanías
A good selection of ceramics and glass, centrally situated near the top of the Born.
✉ **Carrer Unió 13** ☎ 724299

La Casa del Olivo
Wonderful olive-carver's workshop in an alley off Carrer Jaume II. The best buy here is salad bowls – they're not cheap but you're paying for old-fashioned craftsmanship.
✉ **Carrer Pescatería Vella 4**
☎ 727025

Centro Pelaires
Wander the back streets of Palma and you come across numerous contemporary art galleries. This is one of the best, featuring work by Mallorcan and international artists.
✉ **Carrer Veri 7** ☎ 720375

Cestería el Centro
Straw baskets, hats and espadrilles in an old family workshop in the Born.
✉ **Passeig des Born 18**
☎ 724533

Fang i Foc
A good range of ceramics from Mallorca and the Spanish mainland.
✉ **Carrer Libertat 29**
☎ 455860

Fet a Mà
As the name implies, everything 'made by hand'. Pottery and glass, both traditional and modern.
✉ **Carrer Sant Miquel 52**
☎ 711095

Herreros de Vicente Juan Ribas
The best place to buy *roba de llengues* patterned cloth in Palma for over a century. There is another *roba de llengues* shop next door.
✉ **Carrer Sant Nicolau 10**
☎ 721773

Majórica
Palma branch of Mallorca's leading artificial-pearl-maker.
✉ **Avinguda Jaume III 11**
☎ 725268

Midge Dalton
Palma's antique shops are perfect for browsing, and this is one of the best.
✉ **Plaça Mercat** ☎ 713360

Natura
Mallorca branch of a Spanish chain specialising in environment-friendly gifts – candles, wood, clothes.
✉ **Passeig des Born 9**
☎ 718252

Orquídea
Cultured pearls – slightly cheaper than its rival Majórica.
✉ **Plaça Rei Joan Carles I 1**
☎ 715797

Persépolis
High-class antiques on Palma's up-market shopping street, a place to browse rather than buy.
✉ **Avinguda Jaume III 23**
☎ 724539

Vidrierías Gordiola
The best selection of glassware in Palma, produced in Algaida.
✉ **Carrer Victoria 2**
☎ 711541

Around the Island

Algaida
Vidrierías Gordiola
Glass factory and museum (➤ 43) in a mock castle near Algaida.
✉ **Carretera Palma–Manacor km19** ☎ **665046**

Inca
Munper
Mallorcan leather is rarely a bargain these days, but this is the place to go for a wide selection of shoes, handbags and belts – the same factory has another shop at Montuïri.
✉ **Carretera Palma–Alcúdia km30** ☎ **881000**

Llucmajor
Casa Ordinas
Busy workshop where a master cutler produces old-fashioned knives and tools at remarkably good prices.
✉ **Carrer Vall 128** ☎ **660580**

Manacor
Majórica
Shop here after touring Mallorca's largest pearl factory (➤ 60).
✉ **Avinguda Majórica 48** ☎ **550200**

OlivArt
Emporium where everything is made from olive wood.
✉ **Carretera Palma–Manacor km45** ☎ **552800**

Orquídea
Large factory shop featuring artificial pearls.
✉ **Carretera Palma–Manacor km30** ☎ **644144**

Pòrtol
Ca's Canonge
Large selection of pottery, especially heavy brown-glazed cooking pots.
✉ **Carrer Trinitat 61** ☎ **602361**

Ca'n Vent
Pòrtol is the best place to buy traditional Mallocan pottery – of two good *ollerías* in the same street, this is the first one you reach.
✉ **Carrer Trinitat 39** ☎ **602456**

Roca Llisa
One of the best places to buy *siurells* (➤ 106).
✉ **Carrer Roca Llisa 26** ☎ **602497**

Santa Maria del Camí
Bujosa
Factory producing the original *roba de llengües* ('cloth of tongues') – a heavy mix of cotton and linen woven into a zigzag pattern on a narrow loom.
✉ **Carretera Inca 77** ☎ **620054**

Ca'n Bernat
Master craftsman's workshop turning out imaginative local pottery.
✉ **Carrer Bartomeu Pasqual** ☎ **621306**

Santanyí
Ceramiques de Santanyí
Innovative ceramic designs based on ancient Mallorcan traditions – a refreshing change from the identical selections elsewhere.
✉ **Carrer Guardia Civil 22** ☎ **163128**

Sóller
Eugenio
Gifts carved out of olive wood – salad bowls, salt-cellars, chess sets.
✉ **Carrer Jerónimo Estades 11A** ☎ **630984**

Wine
Mallorcan wines have been growing in reputation in recent years and several bodegas sell direct to the public. If you are lucky you will be able to taste before you buy. Among the best producers are José L Ferrer at Binissalem (☎ 511050), Miquel Oliver at Petra (☎ 561117) and Jaume Mesquida at Porreres (☎ 647106).

107

Parks, Zoos & Activities

Family Outings

As well as the attractions listed here, children will enjoy visits to La Granja (▶ 57) and to the various caves along the east coast with their phantasmagorical light displays (▶ 21, 54). The Sóller train and tram ride (▶ 71) makes a fun day out, and the beach at Platja de Palma (▶ 64) is very child-friendly with its seafront 'train', shallow water and Red Cross beach stations.

A Warning

The attractions listed on this page are among the most expensive in Mallorca.

The fact is that you can take children anywhere in Mallorca. Like the Spanish and other Mediterranean people, Mallorcans love and indulge children and even if you take an unruly toddler into a first-class restaurant the only request from the waiter is likely to be for a cuddle.

Mallorca is well geared up for family holidays. There are lots of good sandy beaches with safe, shallow water and first-aid stations, and many of the resorts feature activities like crazy golf courses and pony rides. Some hotels have separate children's pools – ask before you go. Many also offer nurseries and baby-sitting services, and programmes of children's entertainments to keep the little ones amused during the day. So have a day off, leave the children behind, and do what you want for a change! If this is important to you, again, check with your hotel or travel agent before you go.

Here is a selection of activities that will appeal to children.

Theme Parks and Waterparks

Binissalem
Aqualandia/El Foro de Mallorca
This children's paradise has a bit of everything – a waterpark, swimming pool and adventure playground, crazy golf and a waxworks museum.
✉ Carretera Palma–Inca km25 ☎ 511228
🕐 May–Sep, daily 10–6

Magaluf
Aquapark
There are pools, slides, a 'water castle' and exciting rides at this long-established waterpark situated on the edge of town. Karting Magaluf can be found adjacent.
✉ Carretera Cala Figuera ☎ 130811 🕐 Jun–Sep, daily 10–6; May–Oct, daily 10–5

Port d'Alcùdia
Hidropark
A water-based theme park with activities for very young children.
✉ Avinguda Tucán ☎ 891672 🕐 May–Oct 10–6

S'Arenal (Platja de Palma)
Aquacity
One of the world's largest water funfairs, with enough thrills and spills to keep little ones happy all day. In addition to the water slides and wave pool there is a mini-zoo, as well as a children's farm, parrot shows and an antique typewriter museum.
✉ End of Palma–S'Arenal motorway ☎ 440000 🕐 May–Sep, daily 10–5; Oct, Sun–Fri 10–5 🚌 23 from Palma via Platja de Palma

Zoos and Animals

Cala Millor
Auto-Safari
Drive-round safari park with giraffes, zebra and monkeys plus a 'baby zoo' with young elephants and reptiles born at the zoo (▶ 45). Arrive early to see the animals feeding.
✉ Carretera Porto Cristo–Son Servera, km5 ☎ 810909 🕐 Apr–Sep, daily 9–7;

Oct–Mar, daily 9–5 🚌 Free bus service from Cala Millor in summer

Magaluf
Nemo Submarines
See the flora and fauna beneath the sea on a 2-hour exploration by mini-submarine from Magaluf. Very expensive.

✉ **Carrer Pedro Vaquer Ramis** ☎ **184132** 🕐 **Several times daily throughout the year**

Portals Nous
Marineland
Entertainment here is provided by the performing dolphins, sea lions and parrots. There is also a penguin house, a reptile house and a large collection of sharks and tropical fish, plus flamingoes, monkeys and an impressive aviary. Children can take a ride on a mock pirate boat and a miniature train. The little ones will love it, but their parents may not – especially if they are fond of dolphins. But whatever you think about animal shows, Marineland is a success – and the crowds it attracts mean that it is generating profits which are then put back into conservation programmes.

✉ **Carrera Palma–Andratx km10** ☎ **675125** 🕐 **Apr–Sep, daily 9:30–7; Oct–Mar, daily 9:30–5:30. Closed mid-Nov to Christmas** 🚌 **From Palma, Palma Nova, Magaluf and Santa Ponça**

Porto Cristo
Acuàrium de Mallorca
Small aquarium with exotic fish from around the world including piranhas and electric eels. Next to the Coves del Drac (▶ 54).

✉ **Carrer Vèlla** ☎ **820971** 🕐 **Apr–Oct, daily 9:30–5; Nov–Mar, daily 11–3**

Horse Riding

Calvià
Pony Club Calvià
Special courses for children are given at this horse riding club.

✉ **Son Punta** ☎ **670401**

Karting

Magaluf
Karting Magaluf
Go-kart track beside Aquapark – leave the teenagers here while the younger ones get wet next door.

✉ **Carretera Cala Figuera** ☎ **131734** 🕐 **May–Oct, daily 10–5**

Mini Golf

Palma Nova
Golf Fantasia
There are mini-golf courses in many of the resorts, but this is one of the best, set amid waterfalls, caves and tropical gardens. There is a choice of three different circuits – or you can play all 54 holes. Even adults will enjoy it.

✉ **Carrer Tenis 3, Palma Nova** ☎ **682349** 🕐 **Mon–Fri 10:30–6; Sat–Sun 10:30–8**

S'Arenal (Platja de Palma)
Golf Fantasia
When you tire of 'fantasy golf' in Palma Nova, you can visit its sister course on the other side of the bay.

✉ **Carretera Arenal 56, S'Arenal** ☎ **263805** 🕐 **Mon–Fri 10:30–6; Sat–Sun 10:30–8**

Looking After Children
Small children are particularly vulnerable to sun and need to be well protected: apply a high-factor sun block regularly, especially after swimming. If you need a child seat in your rented car, be sure to book it in advance and then check it carefully on arrival. The same goes for cots and high-chairs in hotels and apartments. Finally, don't forget to check that your balcony railings are secure.

Theatres, Cinemas & Concerts

What's On?
To find out what's on while you are staying, ask any tourist office for a copy of *Events*, published quarterly in English and German. The *Majorca Daily Bulletin* also has daily listings. A monthly guide to events in Palma is published in Spanish and Catalan and available at tourist offices and hotels. Remember that everything starts late in Mallorca – opera at 9PM, theatre around 10PM and music any time up to midnight.

Palma
ABC
Large cinema on the ring road showing Spanish films plus the latest international releases dubbed into Spanish.
✉ **Avinguda Alexandre Rosselló 38** ☎ **464527**

Auditòrium
Palma's main venue for theatre and concerts.
✉ **Passeig Marítim 18** ☎ **734735**

Castell de Bellver
Outdoor classical concerts in a spectacular setting on summer evenings.
✉ **Parc Bellver** ☎ **730657**

Centre de Cultura Sa Nostra
Regular programme of free events at this arts centre in an old mansion in central Palma.
✉ **Carrer Concepció 12** ☎ **725210**

Salón Rialto
Popular cinema in the nightlife quarter between La Llotja and the Born.
✉ **Carrer Sant Feliu 5** ☎ **721245**

Ses Voltes
Outdoor concerts (jazz, rock or classical) beneath the city walls on summer evenings and Sunday lunchtimes.
✉ **Parc de la Mar** ☎ **714238**

Teatre Municipal
Contemporary drama, dance, ballet and films.
✉ **Passeig Mallorca 9** ☎ **739148**

Teatre Principal
Nineteenth-century theatre with a spring opera season from March to May.
✉ **Carrer Riera 2** ☎ **725548**

Around the Island

Cala Rajada
Jardins Casa March
These gardens and sculpture park make a beautiful setting for a series of evening concerts each July.
✉ **Parc Casa March** ☎ **563033**

Deià
Son Marroig
Concerts on summer evenings in the gardens created by Archduke Ludwig Salvator. Venue for Deià's annual classical music festival.
✉ **Carretera Valldemossa– Deià** ☎ **639158**

Esporles
La Granja
Displays of folk music and dancing on Wednesday and Friday afternoons at this museum of Mallorcan traditions (► 57).
✉ **La Granja** ☎ **610032**

Pollença
Convent Sant Domingo
The cloisters of this 17th-century monastery make a delightful setting for Pollença's international music festival held each summer.
✉ **Carrer Sant Domingo** ☎ **531008 (for festival details)**

Valldemossa
Reial Cartoixa
Chopin festival held each August and occasional evening concerts in the Carthusian monastery at Valldemossa.
✉ **Valldemossa** ☎ **612106**

Bars & Clubs

Resort Bars

Bars in the main resorts change their names and identities so frequently that recommendations are useless – just follow your nose and you will soon find one that you like. Many bars are foreign-owned, with German or British names, imported beer and satellite TV. A stretch of the Platja de Palma is known as *carrer de la cervesa* ('Beer Street') owing to the predominance of German bars; you will find the British equivalent in Magaluf.

Palma

Abaco
Palma's most unusual bar – to be found in a 17th-century palace close to La Llotja (▶ panel).
✉ Carrer Sant Joan 1
☎ 715911 🕐 From 9PM nightly

Barcelona
Cool jazz bar in a basement beside Abaco.
✉ Carrer Apuntadors 5
🕐 From 10PM; live jazz from midnight nightly

La Bodeguita del Medio
Enjoy Cuban food, rum and *salsa* music – an imitation of its Havana namesake. Go late.
✉ Carrer Vallseca 18
☎ 717832 🕐 From 10PM nightly

Cappuccino Grand Café
The huge windows facing the waterfront seem designed for posing. Definitely the in-place to be seen.
✉ Passeig Marítim 1
☎ 282162 🕐 Lunch to late daily

Club de Mar
Where the yachties meet at night. Dress up if you want to be let in.
✉ Moll Pelaires ☎ 403611
🕐 Lunch to late daily

Hogans
Palma's first Irish pub opened in 1996. Occasional Irish fiddling, popular with locals.
✉ Carrer Monsenyor Palmer 2
☎ 289664 🕐 Noon–3AM daily

Made in Brasil
Popular meeting-place for late-night cocktails, smooching and Latin dance.
✉ Passeig Marítim
☎ 454569 🕐 Late

Victoria
Piano-bar for the 20-something fashion conscious.
✉ Passeig Marítim 32
🕐 From 10PM nightly

Near Palma

Abacanto
Cousin of Abaco (▶ above and panel) in a 19th-century mansion on an industrial estate in the suburb of S'Indioteria. It is difficult to find, so take a taxi.
✉ Camí Son Nicolau, S'Indioteria
☎ 430624

Jazz Forum
Mallorca's leading jazz venue. Go late.
✉ Avinguda Joan Miró 292, Cala Major ☎ 404617
🕐 Daily

Wellies
The trendiest of many waterfront bars by the ritzy Puerto Portals marina.
✉ Puerto Portals marina, Portals Nous ☎ 676444
🕐 Noon–2AM daily

Abaco
Push open a heavy wooden door in Palma's busy nightlife quarter and you enter a different world. Huge baskets of fruit cascade onto the floor; there are fresh flowers everywhere, and a subtle hint of incense. You sip fruit cocktails by candlelight, whilst listening to classical music, then wander into the courtyard with its fountains and caged birds. The drinks are expensive, but everyone should go once.

Discos & Dinner Shows

Dinner Shows
A recent arrival in Mallorca is the 'themed' dinner show and spectacle, which can be anything from folklore and flamenco dancing to a medieval banquet complete with jousting and serving wenches. These shows are basically aimed at tour groups; you can book at any resort hotel. Don't go unless you are prepared to abandon your inhibitions and join in the fun.

Discos

Palma

Clan
Late-night dancing for young and old beneath the windmills overlooking the harbour.
✉ **Plaça del Vapor, Es Jonquet**
☎ **458669**

Pacha
Young and trendy club where Palma's teenagers come to bop the night away
✉ **Passeig Marítim 42**
☎ **737788** 🕐 **10PM to late; nightly in summer, Thu–Sat in winter**

Tito's
Not quite as young as nearby Pacha. There are six bars, a laser show and fantastic views over Palma bay. There is a second entrance via outdoor lifts from Passeig Marítim.
✉ **Plaça Gomila 3** ☎ **730017**
🕐 **11PM–5AM; nightly in summer, Thu–Sat in winter**

Around the Island

BCM
Europe's largest and probably loudest disco, with laser shows, banks of video screens, a swimming pool and room for 4,000 people. The upper level is for the young-and-trendy crowd, while the over-30s gather downstairs. Big-name international stars give live shows here throughout the summer season.
✉ **Avinguda S'Olivera, Magaluf** 🕐 **10PM–5AM; nightly in summer, weekends in winter**

Menta
Designed like a Roman temple around an open-air pool, it honours Alcúdia's history each May with a 'Roman orgy'.
✉ **Avinguda Tucán, Port d'Alcúdia**

Dinner Shows

Around the Island

Casino Mallorca
A choice of gambling in the casino (passport and smart dress required), or the Paladium dinner show with dancing.
✉ **Urbanización Sol de Mallorca, Magaluf** ☎ **454508**
🕐 **Casino 8PM–4AM nightly; show 10PM nightly in summer, Tue, Thu, Sat in winter**

El Dorado
Themed show in a mock-up Wild West town, part of a lively 'entertainment centre' with several discos, restaurants and bars.
✉ **Carretera Cala Figuera, Magaluf** ☎ **131203**
🕐 **8PM–4AM nightly in summer**

Es Fogueró
Flamenco, ballet and cabaret performances.
✉ **Carretera Palma–Santanyí, km11** ☎ **262745** 🕐 **Mon only, dinner from 8, show 10**

Pirate Adventure
Yo-ho-ho and a bundle of fun on a mock pirate ship – with plenty of audience participation required. Don't say you weren't warned!
✉ **Carretera La Porrassa, Magaluf** ☎ **130411** 🕐 **8–12 nightly in summer**

Son Amar
Spanish and Hungarian dancing plus lion-tamers and performing horses.
✉ **Carretera Palma–Sóller, km11** ☎ **753614** 🕐 **Apr–Oct, dinner from 8, show 9**

Golf Courses

Palma
Son Vida
Mallorca's first golf course opened in 1964 on an exclusive estate above Palma. Par 72. There are two five-star hotels near by.
✉ **Urbanización Son Vida**
☎ **791210**

Around the Island

Cala Millor
Son Servera
Nine-hole course amid pine woods by the sea. Par 72.
✉ **Urbanización Costa dels Pins, 6km from Cala Millor**
☎ **567802**

Capdepera
Canyamel
Testing 18-hole course with small greens, sloping fairways and sea breezes. Par 72.
✉ **Urbanización Canyamel**
☎ **564457**

Roca Viva
Six lakes and large, fast greens on this 18-hole course beside the road to Artà. Par 72.
✉ **Carretera Artà–Capdepera**
☎ **565875**

S'Era de Pula
Mallorca's newest course, opened in 1995 between Capdepera and Cala Millor. Par 71, 18 holes.
✉ **Carretera Son Servera–Capdepera, km3**
☎ **817034**

Llucmajor
Son Antem
Wide fairways, fast greens and hidden water hazards on this 18-hole course, opened in 1994. Par 72.
✉ **3km outside Llucmajor on the PM602 to Palma** ☎ **180094**

Magaluf
Poniente
Long and difficult 18-hole course. Lots of lakes and bunkers, this is good for experienced golfers. Par 72.
✉ **Carretera Cala Figuera**
☎ **130148**

Pollença
Pollensa
A tight 9-hole course, with small greens and narrow fairways this course is set on a hill with views out to sea. Par 70.
✉ **2km outside Pollença on Palma road** ☎ **533216**

Porto Colom
Vall d'Or
Nine holes opened in 1985, and nine more holes opened in 1992. Set among pine trees close to the east coast. Par 71.
✉ **Just inland from Porto Colom on the Porto Cristo–Santanyí road** ☎ **837068**

Santa Ponça
Santa Ponça
This is the venue for the Balearic Open and features long, wide fairways in the midst of open countryside dotted with almond trees. Par 72.
✉ **Urbanización Novo Santa Ponça** ☎ **690211**

Ses Illetes
Real Golf de Bendinat
Short 9-hole course on an exclusive estate above the bay of Palma. It is set in an attractive valley with pine, almond and olive trees, but this course will pose little challenge to experienced golfers. Par 68.
✉ **Urbanización Bendinat, between Ses Illetes and Portals Nous** ☎ **405200**

Golf in Mallorca
In 1976 there were two golf courses in Mallorca; now there are 11 and more are being built. All are open throughout the year, providing a refuge for golfers fleeing frost and winter greens elsewhere. The typical cost of a round is 6,000–8,000 pesetas, though this is much reduced if you come on a golfing package holiday. Don't forget to bring a handicap certificate.

Watersports

Sailing in Mallorca
Mallorca has 41 marinas, 30 *clubs nautics* and mooring for 10,000 yachts. Yachts can be chartered locally and most marinas also have facilities for water-skiing and windsurfing. Highlights of the sailing year include the King's Cup in August, the Princess Sofía trophy at Easter, and the Rei en Jaume regatta in July when a flotilla of yachts will re-create the 185-km journey made by Jaume the Conqueror when he landed at Santa Ponça in 1229.

Pedal Boating
Pedal boats are available for hire (usually from beach bars) at most of the bigger resorts. This includes all those in the bay of Palma as well as Cala Millor, Cala d'Or and Porto Cristo on the east coast.

Sailing

Baleares Yacht Charter
For information on chartering a boat, with or without a crew.
☎ 727986

Escuela Nacional de Vela Calanova
The national sailing school in Cala Major runs courses as well as giving advice on all aspects of sailing in and around Mallorca.
✉ Avinguda Joan Miró, Cala Major ☎ 402512

Sail and Surf Pollença
Prestigious sailing club and school on the northeast coast. Instruction is available both for beginners and for the more advanced sailor.
✉ Platja de la Gola, Port de Pollença ☎ 865346

Cala d'Or Marina
☎ 657070

Port d'Andratx Marina
☎ 672337

Port de Pollença Marina
☎ 864635

Puerto Portals Marina (Portals Nous)
☎ 676300

Scuba Diving

Federació Balear di Actividades Subacuáticas
The clear waters around Mallorca are the perfect place for diving, especially in the small, shallow coves of the south and east coasts. The federation is available to give information and advice on all aspects of diving in Mallorca.
✉ Carrer Pere d'Alcàntara Penya 13, Palma ☎ 463315

Aqua Marine Diving
✉ Port d'Andratx ☎ 674376

Escuba Palma
✉ Vía Jaume I 84, Santa Ponça ☎ 694968

Tritón
✉ Carrer Roger de Llúria 4A, Palma ☎ 456125

Unidad Costa Norte
✉ Port Adriano, El Toro, Santa Ponça ☎ 102676

Water-skiing
Water-skiing equipment can be hired on the major beaches, including Cala Millor, Can Picafort, Formentor, Magaluf, Palma Nova, Peguera, Platja de Palma, Port d'Alcúdia and Santa Ponça.

Ski Club Calanova
✉ Carrer Condor 22, Son Ferrer, Santa Ponça ☎ 100328 (also in Magaluf: ☎ 130965)

Windsurfing
There are schools at several of the larger resorts and it is also possible to hire equipment without tuition. Beaches where windsurfing is available include Cala Millor, Cala d'Or, Can Picafort, Formentor, Magaluf, Palma Nova, Peguera, Platja de Palma, Port d'Alcúdia, Port de Pollença, Port de Sóller, Portals Nous and Santa Ponça.

Spectator Sports

Bullfighting

Bullfighting is considered an art form as much as a sport; the leading *matadors* are national celebrities and there are fights most days on TV. A bullfight begins with a horseback procession, or *corrida*, followed by the fight itself; the bull is softened up by *picadores* and then the *matador* moves in for the kill. Many foreigners detest the spectacle – but it is undoubtedly an important aspect of Spanish culture.

Palma
Plaça de Toros
Bullfights are held in this 1929 bullring between March and October. Choose between a seat in the sun (*sol*) or the shade (*sombra*).
✉ **Avinguda Gaspar Bennuzar Arquitecte** ☎ **755245**

Around the Island
Plaça de Toros, Alcúdia
To see some of the drama without the blood, come here for one of the mock bullfights, held on Thursday evenings in summer.
☎ **547903**
Plaça de Toros, Felanitx
☎ **580557**

Plaça de Toros, Inca
☎ **500087**

Plaça de Toros, Muro
This bullring was built in 1910 inside its own quarry of white stone.
☎ **537329**

Cricket

Around the Island
Magaluf Cricket Club
Cricket has been kept determinedly going by a group of British ex-pats in Mallorca, who play local and visiting sides on their ground in Magaluf.
☎ **682880**

Football

Palma
Estadi Lluis Sitjar
The home of Real Mallorca FC. Matches are played on alternate Sunday afternoons between September and March.
✉ **Plaça Barcelona**
☎ **452111**

Greyhound-racing

Palma
Canódromo Balear
Races from 4:30 every afternoon except Wednesday.
✉ **Camí de Jesus** ☎ **290012**

Horse-racing

Palma
Hipódromo Son Pardo
Europe's first floodlit racecourse opened in 1965. Trotting races (*carreras*) are held around a 1-km track at 4:30 on Sundays in winter and 9 on Friday evenings in summer. Trotting is a form of racing in which the jockey sits in a small cart behind the horse and must prevent the horse from breaking into a gallop. It has been popular in Mallorca and Menorca for at least 200 years. If you go to a race meeting, remember that betting is an essential part of the process.
✉ **Carretera Palma–Sóller, km3** ☎ **754031**

Around the Island
Hipódromo Manacor
✉ **Carretera Palma–Artà, km50**
☎ **550023**

Tiro Con Honda (Slingshot)

Livy wrote of Balearic slingshot throwers being employed as mercenaries during Hannibal's crossing of the Alps in 218 BC; a statue of a Balearic slinger in the S'Hort del Rei gardens in Palma is a tribute to their importance in Mallorcan history. The art of the slingshot has recently been revived; to see today's slingers, contact the Club de Honderos, ✉ Bar España, Carrer Oms 20, Palma (☎ 726250).

What's On When

Mallorcan Festivals

Find yourself swept along by the atmosphere of a traditional *festa* and you will get a completely different picture of Mallorca. Most are religious in origin and a few date back to the time of the Christian conquest. Every town and village has its saint's day, whose eve (*revelta*) is marked by a *verbena*, a street party with music, dancing, fireworks and fancy dress. Battles are acted out between devils and heroic women, or Christians and Moors; people prance about as horses, and a good time is had by all.

January

Cabalgata de los Reyes Magos (5 Jan): The Three Kings arrive by boat in Palma to distribute gifts to the city's children.
Sant Antoni Abat (16–17 Jan): Processions of pets and farm animals in Palma, Artà and Sa Pobla.
Sant Sebastià (19 Jan): Bonfires and barbecues in Palma's squares.

February

Sa Rúa (final weekend before Lent): Carnival held in Palma and elsewhere on the last weekend before Lent. It is marked by bonfires, fancy dress and processions of decorated floats. In Montuïri the Carnival is known as *Darres Dies* (Last Days).

March/April

Semana Santa (Holy Week): A week of solemn Easter preparation begins on Palm Sunday, when palm and olive branches are blessed at churches across the island before being taken home to adorn front doors. During Holy Week there are processions every day in Palma; the biggest procession is on Maundy Thursday. Other towns and villages have their own processions too. On the evening of Good Friday a figure of Christ is lowered from his cross in Pollença and carried down the Calvary steps in silence. A similar event takes place on the church steps in Felanitx.

May

Moros i Cristians (8–10 May): Mock battles between heroes and infidels in Sóller, commemorating a 1561 battle in which local women helped to defeat a band of Turkish pirates.

June

Sant Pere (28–9 Jun): Processions of fishing boats in Palma, Port d'Andratx and Port d'Alcúdia in honour of the patron saint of fishermen.

July

La Virgen del Carmen (16 Jul): Processions of boats in the island's ports, including Cala Rajada, Port de Pollença and Port de Sóller.
Santa Catalina Thomás (27–8 Jul): Homage to Mallorca's patron saint in her home town of Valldemossa.

August

Sant Bartomeu (24 Aug): Devil-dancing in Montuïri at one of Mallorca's oldest festivals.
Sant Agustí (28 Aug): *Cavallets* dances in Felanitx, with children dressed up as cardboard horses being chased by giants to the accompaniment of bagpipes, flutes and drums.

September/October

Harvest festivals including a melon festival in Vilafranca de Bonany (second Sun in Sep), a wine fair in Binissalem (last Sun in Sep), and a *botifarró* (blood sausage) festival in Sant Joan (third Sun in Oct).

December

Festa de l'Estendard (31 Dec): Palma commemmorates the anniversary of the Christian conquest with a procession from the town hall to Mass at the cathedral.

Practical
Matters

GMT
12 noon

Mallorca
1PM

Germany
1PM

USA (NY)
7AM

Netherlands
1PM

Rest of Spain
1PM

BEFORE YOU GO

WHAT YOU NEED

		UK	Germany	USA	Netherlands	Spain
●	Required					
○	Suggested					
▲	Not required					
Passport/National Identity Card		●	●	●	●	▲
Visa		▲	▲	▲	▲	▲
Onward or Return Ticket		○	○	●	○	○
Health Inoculations		▲	▲	▲	▲	▲
Health Documentation (► 123, Health)		●	●	●	●	▲
Travel Insurance		○	○	○	○	○
Driving Licence (national with Spanish translation or International)		●	●	●	●	●
Car Insurance Certificate		●	●	●	●	○
Car Registration Document		●	●	●	●	○

WHEN TO GO

Palma

 High season

 Low season

14°C	15°C	17°C	19°C	22°C	26°C	29°C	29°C	27°C	23°C	18°C	15°C
JAN	FEB	MAR	APR	MAY	JUN	JUL	AUG	SEP	OCT	NOV	DEC

 Very wet   Wet   Cloud   Sun   Showers/Sun

TOURIST OFFICES

In the UK
Spanish Tourist Office
57–8 St James's Street
London SW1A 1LD
☎ 0171 499 0901
Fax: 0171 629 4257
(Due to move in the near future – new address not known.)

In the USA
Tourist Office of Spain
666 Fifth Avenue 35th
New York
NY 10103
☎ 212/265 8822
Fax: 212/265 8864

POLICE (POLICÍA NACIONAL) 091

FIRE (BOMBEROS) 080 (PALMA); 085 (ELSEWHERE)

AMBULANCE (AMBULÀNCIA) 061

RED CROSS (CRUZ ROJA) 295000 (PALMA)

WHEN YOU ARE THERE

ARRIVING

Spain's national airline, Iberia (☎ 901 333222), has scheduled flights to Palma's Son Sant Joan Airport from major Spanish and European cities, but charter flights are much cheaper. Ferry services operate from the Spanish mainland, France and Italy to Palma.

Son Sant Joan Airport Kilometres to city centre	**Journey times**	
	🚶	N/A
11 kilometres	🚌	30 minutes
	🚗	15 minutes

Palma Ferry Terminal Kilometres to city centre	**Journey times**	
	🚶	N/A
4 kilometres	🚌	30 minutes
	🚗	10 minutes

MONEY

Spain's currency is the peseta, issued in notes of 1,000, 2,000, 5,000 and 10,000 pesetas and coins of 5, 10, 25, 50, 100, 200 and 500 pesetas. A one-peseta coin still exists but most bills are rounded down to the nearest 5 pesetas. Travellers' cheques are accepted by most hotels, shops and restaurants in lieu of cash, although the rate of exchange may be less favourable than in banks. Travellers' cheques in pesetas are the most convenient. Banks can be found in most towns in Mallorca and handle travellers' cheques, Eurocheques and give advances on credit cards.

TIME

Like the rest of Spain, Mallorca is one hour ahead of Greenwich Mean Time (GMT+1), but from late March until late September, summer time (GMT+2) operates.

CUSTOMS

 YES

Goods Obtained Duty Free Inside the EU or Goods Bought Outside the EU (Limits):
Alcohol (over 22° vol): 1L *or*
Alcohol (not over 22° vol): 2L *and*
Still table wine: 2L
Cigarettes: 200 *or*
Cigars: 50 *or*
Tobacco: 250gms
Perfume: 50gms
Toilet water: 250ml
Goods Bought Duty and Tax Paid Inside the EU (Guidance Levels):
Alcohol (over 22° vol): 10L *and*
Alcohol (not over 22° vol): 20L *and*
Wine (max 60L sparkling): 90L *and* Beer: 110L
Cigarettes: 800 *and*
Cigars: 200 *and*
Tobacco: 1kg
Perfume: no limit
Toilet water: no limit
Visitors must be 17 and over.

 NO

Drugs, firearms, ammunition, offensive weapons, obscene material, unlicensed animals.

UK	Germany	USA	Netherlands
☎ 712445	☎ 722371	☎ 722660	☎ 716493

WHEN YOU ARE THERE

TOURIST OFFICES

Mallorca Tourist Board

● Fomento del Turismo de
  Mallorca
  Carrer de Constitució 1
  Palma 07001
  ☎ 725396

**Local Tourist Offices
(Oficinas de Información
Turística – OIT)**

Palma

● Carrer de Sant Domingo 11
  Palma 07001
  ☎ 724090

● Caseta Plaza España
  Palma 07002
  ☎ 711527

Palma Nova

● Passeig de la Mar 13
  Calvià 07181
  ☎ 682365

Port d'Alcúdia

● Carretera Artà 68
  Alcúdia 07410
  ☎ 892615

Port de Pollença

● Carretera de Formentor 31
  Pollença 07470
  ☎ 865467

Sóller

● Plaça de Sa Constitució 1
  Sóller 07100
  ☎ 630200

Other offices include: Cala
d'Or, Cala Millor, Cala Rajada,
Cala Sant Vicenç, Ca'n
Picafort, Colònia de Sant
Jordi, Magaluf, Peguera,
Platja de Murro, Port de
Sóller, Porto Cristo, S'Arenal,
Ses Illetes, and Santa Ponça.

NATIONAL HOLIDAYS

J	F	M	A	M	J	J	A	S	O	N	D
2		(2)	(2)	1			1		1	1	3

1 Jan	New Year's Day
6 Jan	Epiphany
Mar/Apr	Good Friday, Easter Monday
1 May	Labour Day
15 Aug	Assumption of the Virgin
12 Oct	National Day
1 Nov	All Saints' Day
6 Dec	Constitution Day
8 Dec	Feast of the Immaculate Conception
25 Dec	Christmas Day

Many shops and offices close for longer periods
around Christmas and Easter, as well as for the
festivals of Corpus Christi in May/June and Sant
Jaume on 25 July.

OPENING HOURS

○ Shops	● Churches
● Offices	◐ Museums
● Banks	◐ Pharmacies

8AM 9AM 10AM 12PM 1PM 2PM 4PM 6PM 8PM

☐ Day	☐ Midday
☐ Evening	

In addition to the times shown above, large
department stores, as well as supermarkets and
shops in tourist resorts may open outside these times,
especially in summer. In general, pharmacies, banks
and shops close on Saturday afternoon, though banks
stay open until 4:30PM Monday to Thursday, October
to May, but close Saturday, June to September.

The opening times of museums is just a rough guide;
some are open longer hours in summer while hours
are reduced in winter. Some museums close at
weekends or another day in the week.

DRIVE ON THE
RIGHT

TOILETS
FREE

PUBLIC TRANSPORT

 Trains There are two railway lines in Mallorca, connecting Palma to Inca and Sóller. Palma's two stations are close together beside Plaça d'Espanya. Fast trains to Inca take 35 minutes and leave at least hourly throughout the day (first train 6am), stopping at Marratxí, Santa Maria del Camí, Consell, Binissalem, Alaró and Lloseta (information: ☎ 752245). The train journey to Sóller (► 71) takes 55 minutes and is tremendous fun. Five trains leave Palma daily, the first at 8AM (information: ☎ 752051).

 Island Buses An efficient system of buses connects Palma to all the main towns in Mallorca, and there are also a number of more local routes. Most buses out of Palma leave from the Plaça d'Espanya and you can pick up a timetable from the tourist information kiosk on the square. Most services operate at a reduced level from November to April. For information, contact Conselleria Transports, Plaça d'Espanya, Palma (☎ 753445).

 Boat Trips The best way to see the coastline, and particularly reach some of the remoter coves which are inaccessible by road, is by boat. One of the most popular trips goes around the northwest coast from Port de Sóller to Sa Calobra – this is one of the few boat trips to fun throughout the year (☎ 753445). There are numerous summer excursions (contact tourist offices for details).

 Urban Transport Only Palma is large enough to have its own transport system with a web of bus services linking the city centre with the suburbs and tourist resorts around it. Services are run by EMT (☎ 753445). There is also a tram that runs between Sóller and Port de Sóller (journey time 30 minutes).

CAR RENTAL

 The leading international car rental companies have offices at Palma airport and you can book a car in advance (essential in peak periods) either direct or through a travel agent. Local companies offer competitive rates and will usually deliver a car to the airport.

TAXIS

 Taxis can be hired at ranks (indicated by a blue square with a 'T'), on the street (by flagging down those with a green light), or at hotels. They are good value within Palma but expensive over long distances. A list of tariffs is displayed at taxi ranks.

DRIVING

 Speed limits on motorways (*autopistas*): **120kph**

 Speed limits on main roads: **100kph**
Speed limits on minor roads: **90kph**

 Speed limits on urban roads: **60kph**

 Must be worn in front seats at all times and in rear seats where fitted.

 Random breath-testing. Limit: 80 micrograms of alcohol in 100ml of breath.

 Fuel (*gasolina*) is available in four grades: *Super Plus* (98 octane), *Super* (96 octane) and often unleaded (*sin plomo*), *Mezcla* or *Normal* (90 ocatne), and *gasoleo* or *gasoil* (diesel). Petrol stations are normally open 6AM–10PM, and closed Sundays, though larger ones (often self service) are open 24 hours. Most take credit cards. There are few petrol stations in the mountain areas.

 If you break down driving your own car and are a member of an AIT-affiliated motoring club, you can call the Real Automóvil Club de España (☎ 91 593 3333). If the car is hired follow the instructions given in the documentation; most of the international rental firms provide a resue service.

121

PERSONAL SAFETY

The national police force, the Policía Nacional (brown uniforms) keep law and order in urban areas. Some resorts have their own tourist-friendly Policía Turística. If you need a police station ask for *la comisaría*.

To help prevent crime:

- Do not carry more cash than you need.
- Do not leave valuables on the beach or poolside.
- Beware of pickpockets in markets, tourist sights or crowded places.
- Avoid walking alone in dark alleys at night.

Police assistance:
☎ **091**
from any call box

TELEPHONES

A public telephone (*teléfono*) takes 25, 100 and 500-peseta coins (both new and old). A phonecard (*credifone*) is available from post offices and *tabacos* for 1,000 or 2,000 pesetas.

All telephone numbers in the Balearic Islands have the same code (971), so within Mallorca you need dial only the six-figure numbers shown in this guide. To call the operator dial 002.

International Dialling Codes	
From Mallorca (Spain) to:	
UK:	07 44
Germany:	07 49
USA:	07 1
Netherlands:	07 31

POST

Post Offices
Post offices (*correus*) are open as below but some also open in the afternoon and on Saturday morning. The main post office in Palma at Carrer de Constitució 5 is open Monday to Friday 9AM to 9PM (to 2PM Saturday).
Open: 9AM (Mon–Fri)
Closed: 2PM
☎ 721095

ELECTRICITY

The power supply in Mallorca is:
220–225 volts.

Sockets accept two-round-pin-style plugs, so an adaptor is needed for most non-Continental appliances and a transformer for appliances operating on 100–120 volts.

TIPS/GRATUITIES

Yes ✓ No ✗		
Restaurants (if service not included)	✓	10%
Cafés/bars (if service not included)	✓	change
Tour guides	✓	100ptas
Hairdressers	✓	change
Taxis	✓	10%
Chambermaids	✓	100ptas
Porters	✓	100ptas
Theatre/cinema usherettes	✓	change
Cloakroom attendants	✓	change
Toilets	✗	

PHOTOGRAPHY

What to photograph: mountains, hilltop monasteries, pretty mountain villages and attractive harbours.

Best time to photograph: the Mallorcan summer sun can be powerful at the height of the day making photos taken at this time appear 'flat'; it is best to photograph in the early morning or late evening.

Where to buy film: film and camera batteries are readily available from tourist shops and *droguerías*.

HEALTH

Insurance

Nationals of EU and certain other countries can get medical treatment in Spain with the relevant documentation (Form E111 for Britons), although private medical insurance is still advised and is essential for all other visitors.

Dental Services

Dental treatment is not usually available free of charge as all dentists practice privately. A list of *dentistas* can be found in the yellow pages of the telephone directory. Dental treatment should be covered by private medical insurance.

Sun Advice

The sunniest (and hottest) months are July and August with an average of 11 hours sun a day and daytime temperatures of 29°C. Particularly during these months you should avoid the midday sun and use a strong sunblock.

Drugs

Prescription and non-prescription drugs and medicines are available from pharmacies (*farmàcias*), distinguished by a large green cross. They are able to dispense many drugs which would be available only on prescription in other countries.

Safe Water

Tap water is generally safe though it can be heavily chlorinated. Mineral water is cheap to buy and is sold as *con gaz* (carbonated) and *sin gaz* (still). Drink plenty of water during hot weather.

CONCESSIONS

Students Holders of an International Student Identity Card may be able to obtain some concessions on travel, entrance fees etc, but Mallorca is not really geared up for students, it is more suited to families and senior citizens. However, there are two youth hostels on the island, one near Palma and the other outside Alcúdia. Another cheap form of accommodation is to stay in a monastery; just turn up or book ahead.

Senior Citizens Mallorca is an excellent destination for older travellers, especially in winter when the resorts are quieter, prices more reasonable and hotels offer very economical long-stay rates. The best deals are available through tour operators who specialise in holidays for senior citizens.

CLOTHING SIZES

Mallorca (Spain)	UK	Rest of Europe	USA	
46	36	46	36	Suits
48	38	48	38	Suits
50	40	50	40	Suits
52	42	52	42	Suits
54	44	54	44	Suits
56	46	56	46	Suits
41	7	41	8	Shoes
42	7.5	42	8.5	Shoes
43	8.5	43	9.5	Shoes
44	9.5	44	10.5	Shoes
45	10.5	45	11.5	Shoes
46	11	46	12	Shoes
37	14.5	37	14.5	Shirts
38	15	38	15	Shirts
39/40	15.5	39/40	15.5	Shirts
41	16	41	16	Shirts
42	16.5	42	16.5	Shirts
43	17	43	17	Shirts
34	8	34	6	Dresses
36	10	36	8	Dresses
38	12	38	10	Dresses
40	14	40	12	Dresses
42	16	42	14	Dresses
44	18	44	16	Dresses
38	4.5	38	6	Shoes
38	5	38	6.5	Shoes
39	5.5	39	7	Shoes
39	6	39	7.5	Shoes
40	6.5	40	8	Shoes
41	7	41	8.5	Shoes

WHEN DEPARTING

● Remember to contact the airport on the day prior to leaving to ensure the flight details are unchanged.

● If travelling by ferry you must check in no later than the time specified on the ticket.

● Spanish customs officials are usually polite and normally willing to negotiate.

LANGUAGE

The language that you hear on the streets is most likely to be Mallorquín, a version of Catalan, which itself shares features with both French and Spanish but sounds nothing like either and is emphatically a language, not a dialect. Catalan and Spanish both have official status on Mallorca, and though Spanish will certainly get you by (it is still the language used by Mallorcans to address strangers), it is useful to know some Catalan if only to understand all those street signs which are being slowly replaced in Catalan.

hotel	*hotel*	chambermaid	*cambrera*
bed and breakfast	*llit i berenar*	bath	*bany*
single room	*habitació senzilla*	shower	*dutxa*
double room	*habitació doble*	toilet	*toaleta*
one person	*una persona*	balcony	*balcó*
one night	*una nit*	key	*clau*
reservation	*reservas*	lift	*ascensor*
room service	*servei d'habitació*	sea view	*vista al mar*

bank	*banc*	credit card	*carta de crèdit*
exchange office	*oficina de canvi*	exchange rate	*tant per cent*
post office	*correus*	commission	*comissió*
coin	*moneda*	charge	
banknote	*bitllet de banc*	cashier	*caixer*
cheque	*xec*	change	*camvi*
travellers' cheque	*xec de viatge*	foreign currency	*moneda estrangera*

café	*cafè*	starter	*primer plat*
pub/bar	*celler*	main course	*segón plat*
breakfast	*berenar*	dessert	*postres*
lunch	*dinar*	bill	*cuenta*
dinner	*sopar*	beer	*cervesa*
table	*mesa*	wine	*vi*
waiter	*cambrer*	water	*aigua*
waitress	*cambrera*	coffee	*café*

aeroplane	*avió*	single ticket	*senzill-a*
airport	*aeroport*	return ticket	*anar i tornar*
train	*tren*	non-smoking	*no fumar*
bus	*autobús*	car	*cotxe*
station	*estació*	petrol	*gasolina*
boat	*vaixell*	bus stop	*la parada*
port	*port*	how do I get to...?	*per anar a...?*
ticket	*bitllet*	where is...?	*on és...?*

yes	*si*	you're welcome	*de res*
no	*no*	how are you?	*com va?*
please	*per favor*	do you speak English?	*parla anglès?*
thank you	*gràcies*		
welcome	*de res*	I don't understand	*no ho entenc*
hello	*hola*		
goodbye	*adéu*	how much?	*quant es?*
good morning	*bon dia*	open	*obert*
good afternoon	*bona tarda*	closed	*tancat*
goodnight	*bona nit*	today	*avui*
excuse me	*perdoni*	tomorrow	*demà*

INDEX

Acknowledgements
The Automobile Assocation wishes to thank the following photographers, libraries and
associations for their assistance in the preparation of this book:

BRIDGEMAN ART LIBRARY 56 La Vent Parmi Les Roseaux, 1971, by Joan Miró (Marlborough
Graphics, London); MARY EVANS PICTURE LIBRARY 11, 14b; MRI BANKERS' GUIDE TO
FOREIGN CURRENCY 119; NATURE PHOTOGRAPHERS 13 (Kevin Carlson); SPECTRUM
COLOUR LIBRARY F/Cover: Beach near Alcúdia, Orange blossom, B/Cover: pottery, 7, 17, 20,
24/5, 26, 48, 58/9, 63; WORLD PICTURES F/Cover: folklore

The remaining photographs are held in the Association's own library (AA PHOTO LIBRARY) and
were taken by Peter Baker, with the exception of pages 9a, 15a, 27b, 35, 67, 79, 80, 91b, which
were taken by Wyn Voysey, pages 75, 76, 85, which were taken by H Rainbow, and page 122a
which was taken by James A Tims

Contributors
Copy editor: Audrey Horne Page Layout: Design 23 Verifier: Mary Tisdall
Researcher (Practical Matters): Colin Follett Indexer: Marie Lorimer

Dear Essential Traveller

**Your comments, opinions and recommendations are very
important to us. So please help us to improve our travel
guides by taking a few minutes to complete this simple
questionnaire.**

*You do not need a stamp (unless posted outside the UK). If you do not want to cut this page
from your guide, then photocopy it or write your answers on a plain sheet of paper.*

Send to: **The Editor, AA World Travel Guides,
FREEPOST SCE 4598, Basingstoke RG21 4GY.**

Your recommendations...

We always encourage readers' recommendations for restaurants, nightlife
or shopping – if your recommendation is used in the next edition of the
guide, we will send you a *FREE* AA *Essential* **Guide** of your choice.
Please state below the establishment name, location and your reasons
for recommending it.

_____

_____

_____

_____

Please send me **AA *Essential*** _____

(see list of titles inside the front cover)

About this guide...

Which title did you buy?
 AA *Essential* _____

Where did you buy it? _____

When? m m / y y

Why did you choose an AA *Essential* Guide? _____

_____

_____

_____

_____

Did this guide meet your expectations?
 Exceeded ☐ Met all ☐ Met most ☐ Fell below ☐
 Please give your reasons _____

_____

_____

_____

continued on next page...

Were there any aspects of this guide that you particularly liked? _____
_____
_____
_____

Is there anything we could have done better? _____
_____
_____
_____
_____

About you…

Name (*Mr/Mrs/Ms*) _____
    Address _____
_____
_____ Postcode _____
    Daytime tel nos _____

Which age group are you in?
    Under 25 ☐ 25–34 ☐ 35–44 ☐ 45–54 ☐ 55–64 ☐ 65+ ☐

How many trips do you make a year?
    Less than one ☐ One ☐ Two ☐ Three or more ☐

Are you an AA member? Yes ☐ No ☐

About your trip…

When did you book? m m / y y   When did you travel? m m / y y
How long did you stay? _____
Was it for business or leisure? _____
Did you buy any other travel guides for your trip?
    If yes, which ones? _____
_____

Thank you for taking the time to complete this questionnaire. Please send
it to us as soon as possible, and remember, you do not need a stamp
(*unless posted outside the UK*).

Happy Holidays!